THE UNSEEN WAR IN IRAQ

THE UNSEEN WAR IN IRAQ:
INSURGENTS IN THE SHADOWS

.

by

Richard Saccone

www.hollym.com

HOLLYM INTERNATIONAL CORP.
Elizabeth, NJ

The Unseen War in Iraq: Insurgents in the Shadows

Published by Hollym International Corp.
Elizabeth, NJ USA
www.hollym.com   email: contact@hollym.com

The views expressed in this book are solely those of the author and do not necessarily reflect the views and opinions of the publisher or its employees.

Hollym International Corp. bears no responsibility for the persistence or accuracy of URLs for external or third-party internet websites referred to in this publication and does not guarantee that any content on such websites is, or will remain, accurate or appropriate.

ISBN: 978-1-56591-134-5
Library of Congress Control Number: 2008933827

Cover Design by TurnThru Creative
www.turnthru.com

Printed in the United States of America

TABLE OF CONTENTS

	Introduction	1
1	The Nightmare that is Reality	6
2	Abu Ghraib Prison	16
	Red Cross Visit	31
3	Our Iraqi Hosts	33
4	Translators	53
5	Prison Informants	60
6	Torture and Coercion	67
7	Interrogation	99
8	Mosul	113
9	Foreign Contract Workers	124
10	The Kidnapping of Fatih	132
11	Turkish Mafia on Base	145
12	Rampant Fake Identification	155
13	The Rasputin of Interpreters	170
14	The One that Got Away	183
15	Abdul Sulayman	194
16	A Suspicious Kurd	205
17	Insurgent Cell Leader	215
18	Possible VBIED?	225
	Ramazan	226
19	Mole Among Prison Terps	231
20	Fence Thieves	241
21	Suspicious Syrian Travel	254
22	Iraqi Police	260
23	PKK in Northern Iraq	266
24	U.S. Contractors	269
25	U.S. Military	279
	Final Thoughts	282
	Acknowledgments	283
	List of Abbreviations	284
	About the Author	286

INTRODUCTION

Naturally, among the cascade of books published on the war in Iraq, most focus on the actual warfare, either the initial military-to-military combat or the in your face fighting with the insurgency. Of course, that subject is the most familiar to readers exposed to the war on television in all its action combat glory. Infantry units clearing a village house by house, raiding homes in search of insurgents, taking and returning fire—these all reinforce the romantic notions of war that Americans are most accustomed to and what we like to learn more about. Young men who couldn't make it to the battlefield want to live vicariously the lives of those soldiers on the frontlines and know what it means to come under fire.

After the military-to-military combat concluded in Iraq with a decisive victory for the U.S. and Coalition Forces, the insurgency began almost immediately. Our military, ever concerned about captives who could expect mistreatment, even beheading at the hands of radical Islamists, became a hunker-down army. The military concentrated itself within fortified bases and sallied forth on patrol to meet the enemy in strength then returned to the safety of secured installations. Few persons were authorized to travel outside

1

the protective wire of the base other than combat patrols, engineers and civil affairs personnel who drew the mission of meeting community officials and winning hearts and minds of the local populace. Military leaders became extremely cautious about protecting personnel. Gone were the days of wandering into town for a drink or dinner. The danger of kidnapping or bombing rendered such activities too perilous. Military and civilian personnel traveled between bases in armed convoys fortified like prickly porcupines to deter enemy attack. Although the bases themselves became targets for mortars and indirect fire from the insurgency, for the most part, the war continued outside the wire, outside the confines of the perimeter of the base.

But the insurgency proved a resilient bunch, constantly adapting to changes in the battlefield, themselves changing to strike a blow however possible to the U.S. military. They developed ways to infiltrate the very sanctuaries where the military felt most safe. Learning to exploit vulnerabilities in U.S. defenses, it did not take long for insurgents to terrorize the U.S. in the places they felt most secure—their homes.

On 21 December 2004, the men and women assigned to Forward Operating Base (FOB) Marez in Mosul, the third largest city in Iraq, dined happily in the tent-like facility known in military jargon as the DFAC (dining facility). That afternoon, a young Iraqi man calmly walked into the midst of the soldiers, said a prayer and blew himself up killing 22 Americans and wounding 60. The shock that explosion sent through the military and the press reached all the way to America in a very short time. While it represented only a small portion of the threat posed to our troops, this suicide bombing illustrated all too well the problem Americans faced inside the wire. It is quite unnerving for soldiers to return from combat operations to a place they believe is a safe haven only to discover it is just another danger zone. In fact, it is unnerving to the point of unacceptability. So, how do we secure our installations in a war zone? Just lock them down you say instinctively. Unfortunately, the problem is more complex than a first glance reveals.

Military installations are sometimes shared with the Iraqis, the very force we are training to assume responsibility for their own country. The problem of insurgent penetration of the Iraqi forces is real and will be discussed in a later section. In addition, U.S. forces rely on local national translators, many of whom live on the base for their own security. If their collaboration with the U.S. were discovered, they would be killed in a most gruesome way, but there are certainly spies among them. Add to that number, the thousands of contract employees and local labor with access to the base, picking up the chores once performed by soldiers but in the modern leaner, meaner military became contracted services, like DFAC duty, manual labor, light construction, maintenance, and a host of other duties. Foreign nationals with access to a base the size of Marez can total more than several thousand, the faces of those people change constantly and they quit or disappear for a variety of reasons. Insurgents are clever enough to realize that of several thousand possible chances to infiltrate the base, surely they can succeed in at least one or two instances. Penetration can yield valuable intelligence for the insurgency as well as providing a stealth force to strike terror at the proper time. Most people still harbor the Cold War image of espionage, men in dark coats armed with special cameras stealing classified information. In the war zone, basic observable knowledge can be more helpful to the insurgency. How many vehicles in a convoy, how many gun trucks, from which gate do the convoys depart, what time do they leave? What are the signs they are preparing to depart? What is their destination? How are they armed? It does not take a sophisticated individual to learn this type of info. It does take access.

Sifting through this human haystack searching for the proverbial insurgent needle is the job of counterintelligence (CI). Skilled CI agents work closely with Force Protection soldiers to identify and eliminate infiltrators and spies before they can damage our forces in the sanctuary of their homes. This battle of trickery and wit is what I refer to as the war inside the wire. As I have mentioned at several staff meetings to combat troops facing bullets every day, "There is a war outside the wire and we fight it every day on patrol, but the enemy is among us. There is another war, inside the wire, that although fought in silence is no less important to your safety. In some ways it is even more important because a man with his guard down is more vulnerable than a soldier prepared to meet

4

his enemy in battle." Sometimes the military leviathan is too busy fighting the war outside the wire to recognize the dangerous one raging within.

Without revealing classified methods that would undermine the CI effort, I will try to expose the reader to the war inside the wire, a war of cloak and dagger and intrigue, a war interesting in its methods and critical to overall success. All of the examples have been modified to dramatize certain philosophical questions or to conceal actual events.

1 THE NIGHTMARE THAT IS REALITY

Boredom overwhelmed the soldier at West gate, one of two entrances directly across from each other separated by an Iraqi highway that effectively split one base into two. West gate served as the vehicle entrance to the east side of the base known as Forward Operating Base (FOB) Diamondback. Its twin on the other side of Sugar Beet Road marked the entrance to FOB Marez. Hundreds of vehicles entered West gate in the two hours the guard stood perfunctorily checking ID cards in the heat of the day, always vigilant for insurgents who might remain concealed among them or indirect fire that could suddenly come from any direction. That day, military convoys arrived from Dohuk with supplies fresh from Turkey, less than 70 miles to the North. Dirt-covered Humvees with machine gun equipped turrets mounted on top lead the convoy, typically followed by 50 tractor-trailer trucks. Some of the goods will supply our base, the rest will standby in the MCT (Movement Control Team) yard until separate convoys are formed heading in all directions to Talafar, Q-West, and Balad, to Camps with names like Sykes, Endurance and Anaconda. Among the drivers of the trailer trucks are Turks, Kurds and Arabs. No one knows who they are exactly. Subcontractors hire them, whoever is willing to run the risk

6

of attack by insurgents on the road from Zahko, on the Iraq border with Turkey, to Mosul. Most drivers are decent souls, just poor men with a family trying to earn a buck. But one among them is not just any shepherd turned trucker. Abdullah Khalid Mohammed is a poor man like the others, yet he has found a way to earn extra money. His friend Said (pronounced in two syllables, sa-eed) is paying him well to enter the U.S. military camp and report back to the insurgency the entire process of entry, including all security procedures. No risk involved. His instructions were to join the convoy as a truck driver and make mental note of security procedures at the numerous checkpoints—the routes, how the trucks are inspected once reaching Mosul, where they park, how they are guarded overnight, how much access to the airfield a driver may have once inside the base. Abdullah has nothing to fear. He is a legitimate driver, but the information he will send back to the insurgency is highly useful. Indeed it is so valuable that the insurgency will pay dearly for it. Not much by American standards, only a few hundred dollars to start, but to Abdullah that amounts to a small fortune. The more detailed the information the more the insurgency will pay. With no job, a third grade education and a large extended family depending on him, Abdullah can earn enough to proudly support his two wives, eight children, and his elderly parents.

Bassam is different. He lives in the village of Abu Sa'if, outside the compound known as FOB Diamondback, the sister base

7

of FOB Marez, which contains the largest airfield in northern Iraq. American soldiers patrol the village, but Bassam keeps a low profile. His Imam advised those who would listen, to smile and wave as the soldiers pass by. Every Friday the same Imam blasts the collaborators in his sermons, condemning all those who work for the American dogs as lower than the very infidels they serve. U.S. soldiers routinely surveyed the mosque for several weeks but failed to gather enough evidence to arrest anyone. Secretly, the Imam meets with a few trusted villagers, including Bassam, and encourages them to obtain employment on the post. "Make friends with the Americans, earn their trust," he urges. "The infidel is weak minded and will reveal what we need to know." With time, the workers will be exposed to information of value to the insurgency. Bits of info here and there… in themselves the pieces are meaningless, but combined they complete a grand picture puzzle.

Bassam is eager to please. Young and impressionable he needs the money and believes the Imam. He is illiterate but the Imam has offered hope for his future reminding him that marriage, money, and respect all spring from devotion to the cause against the infidel. Bassam cues up at the pedestrian gate in the line of day laborers, patiently waiting in the hot sun for someone who needs a man with a strong back to unload pallets, fill sandbags, or perform other menial tasks around post. Several hundred people find work each day this way. Coalition Forces need basic labor and have been pressured by the Iraqi government to hire locals. Despite the security risk to U.S. Forces, politics trumps security. Suddenly, Bassam's name is called. His Iraqi ID is given a token glance by the young soldier at the gate, who does not even drop her feet from on top of the desk as she checks the workers. Bassam eyes the slothful female in disgust thinking to himself, "It is not proper for a woman to work in this manner." She exchanges his Iraqi ID for a red security badge imprinted with bold letters proclaiming, "Escort required." He is in! Now, he only needs to keep his eyes and ears open for information of value as the Imam instructed him. An impatient soldier motions him on the bus with the other laborers. SSGT Jones, who supervises the men, is not worried, smiling at the men as they take their seats. What threat can these men be? They are simple, uneducated he assures himself.

Kemal is a Turkish businessman. He operates the food court on Diamondback, offering burgers, pizza, chicken and Mexican dishes to the troops who enjoy visiting there instead of eating at the DFAC. He staffs the four separate restaurants with Turkish employees recruited from Adana, Turkey. FOB security is strict. Kemal is only allowed a specific number of workers on the FOB at any time but he spots a business opportunity if he acquires additional workers. Always alert for loopholes in the rules, he finds an ingenious solution. Each worker is given a badge with photo upon acceptance to the base. Kemal simply borrows a badge from a worker in the burger bar and meets an illegal worker outside providing him the means to enter the base illegally but undetected.

The method assumes the gate guard will not check each badge closely and generally, the guards do not. Once on the base, the worker is kept out of sight so he is not detected by the patrols that randomly check workers for proper ID. Kemal has smuggled twenty-two people on base and hired them out to other foreign national subcontractors as laborers. Eventually he is caught and banned from the FOB. No matter, the loophole is identified by the insurgency and while security is heightened for a few weeks, it eventually returns to its normal semi-lax state.

On the other side of Mosul sits FOB Courage. As the third largest city in Iraq, Mosul boasts 1.5 million people. The base is situated in such a way that the pedestrian gate is near a busy part of town. Every morning local nationals throng the gate looking for employment with the U.S. This is where the U.S. contractor Titan fishes for perspective applicants to hire as linguists which are in dire need in Iraq. Titan has not been able to fill even half the slots requested by the military and the linguist recruiters are desperate. Hassan, an Arab American working for the contractor, has been told by his boss that if he doesn't recruit more linguist applicants he will be looking for a new job.

Hassan resists, "Look, I have been all over the city. It is hard to find people who will talk to me let alone find ones who speak English."

His boss provides a stern reply, "That's YOUR problem. I pay you well to find linguists—now start producing."

Hassan leaves the office hurt but determined to keep his job. As he heads out the gate to the city he sees the hundreds of people waiting in line for employment. Impulsively he yells out, "Anyone here speak English?" a few hands go up. Hassan waves them over and after a short conversation concludes he has just found four easy recruits.

Linguists earn much more than laborers and the four are happy for the white-collar job that appeared unexpectedly. Allah be praised! The others in line observe quietly. Among them is an informant for the insurgency. "My friends will want to know this," he thinks to himself. Within a few days, the insurgents have planted Salim among those standing at the gate waiting for jobs. Just as expected, Hassan arrives and delivers his usual call for English speakers. Salim raises his hand along with several others.

Hassan motions them closer and poses simple questions in English. "What is your name? Where are you from? Where did you learn to speak English? How many people are in your family?" Salim passes without problem and Hassan quickly welcomes him to his new job as a linguist.

"This was too easy," Salim worries silently. "It must be a trap." Salim follows Hassan into the base. "Where will I work?" he questions.

Hassan is busy filling out paperwork, "Don't worry about that now, we will decide your assignment later."

Salim is content just to have a job with the Coalition Forces. His handlers will be proud of him. In fact, that night they toast his progress at a small gathering in the Nabi Sheet section of Mosul. "Work well my friend," his handler smiles as he pats Salim's shoulder. "Stay in your position for the time being, but at the first opportunity transfer across town to FOB Diamondback. That is where our cause needs you most. We have great plans for you. Allah will bless you for your diligence." Salim is on top of the world. He is earning high pay, about $650 dollars a month, much more than the few dollars a day he would earn on the Iraqi economy. More importantly, he has earned the respect of his handlers, men that have helped his family when he needed help the most. He owes them a debt that cannot be repaid with money.

Then there is Khalid. Growing up in one of Saddam's 75 palaces, Khalid's father rose to become manager of the Palace lake resort visited frequently by Saddam and his family. Khalid grew up with Qusay and Uday, Saddam's barbarous sons. As children they played together. Khalid's father had a wonderful job. Saddam visited the resort only a few months of the year. The rest of the time Khalid's family acted as caretakers and enjoyed the life of the privileged. Khalid met Saddam too many times to count. He grew to love him and appreciate the life his family enjoyed under Saddam's regime. Khalid and his brothers attended the best college in Baghdad and Khalid spoke English well. After the fall of Saddam his life changed, he became a wanted man. Khalid joined the insurgency changing his name and date of birth to disguise his identity. Now, he too had landed a good job as an interpreter for one of the U.S. Army Striker Brigades that patrolled the city. He was loved by the young men in the unit because he was hip to American music and slang. Khalid rose quickly in rank becoming the trusted personal interpreter of the unit commander. Once while on patrol, a Striker was hit by an IED (Improvised Explosive Device) and Khalid helped the soldiers carry the wounded. That clinched it. Khalid had been to battle, taken fire with the men. He was now one of them in their eyes, forging the kind of camaraderie that can only develop between men in combat. But privately Khalid detested his American compatriots. Secretly he longed for the old days under Saddam and the prestige his family once enjoyed. The insurgency promised him a senior position once they had regained power. Khalid maintained his cover as an interpreter, waiting for the right moment when he could betray his oppressor.

Four insurgent leaders gathered in a small room down a narrow alley in Mosul. As they sipped tea Ahmed Hussein brought word directly from Abu Musab Al-Zarqawi himself. "We must attack the infidel on his home ground," he leaned forward and shook both clenched fists as he spoke. "We are ordered to plan an attack on FOB Diamondback. Our cells have infiltrated the base in numbers, the time to strike is now." The others watched silently as he continued, "What is the best place to attack?" Ahmed now searched the eyes of those seated around him looking for answers.

Abass spoke first. "One of our most trusted agents, Khalid, has reported that the dining hall is packed with soldiers at the noon and dinner meals. If we could strike there it would produce many casualties. The gymnasium is another good location because soldiers remove their body armor to exercise. They congregate there in the evenings and a hundred could be killed in an instant." He smiles, proud of his contribution. "I recommend a suicide bomber," the older man smiling reveals a mouth of teeth some black with decay others tipped with gold. "Let us duplicate the bombing of 2004 and send the infidels to the hell they deserve. Allah be praised."

Ahmed interrupted, "We can set off several explosions simultaneously. We will arrange for a few of our day laborers to plant the explosives in appropriate places on post. Abass, can we smuggle explosives onto the post?"

Abass grins as he rocks back then forward, both hands on his knees, "By the prophet, blessings and peace be upon him, we CAN do so. Our drivers can secret the explosives we need into the gravel trucks regularly entering FOB Diamondback. The rocks sufficiently hide the explosives from x-ray and the gravel trucks are rarely checked anyway. The infidel is lazy and our men have earned the confidence of the Americans. That night, our trusted employees on post will transfer the explosives from the MCT yard to a staging area where the laborers may plant them the following day."

"Brilliant," Ahmed is pleased as are the others around the table. "In a few days we will strike multiple points within the soft underbelly of the infidel. Insha Allah (God willing) we will put terror in his heart and drive him from this land forever. Allah be praised."

In unison, they all respond, "Allah be praised."

The danger from insurgents is real and while this scenario is fictional it is based on information from actual insurgent activity. It is not hard to imagine the havoc infiltrators could inflict on the military bases if left unchecked.

2   ABU GHRAIB PRISON

Most people formed their impression of Abu Ghraib prison from the
scandal thrust on them through the nightly news. But few possess a
real sense of life at the infamous Abu G, as it was often called. My
first glimpse came on a convoy as I approached the most famous
prison in the world, looking out the tiny plexiglass window of my
Humvee as we rolled up the highway to the prison. It was hot even
in December and the road on both sides had been cleared of trees to
deny cover to insurgents waiting to ambush convoys traveling along
this busy highway. Security was tight even with the roadsides
cleared back fifty feet or so. Sgt Jones, driving the Humvee,
pointed to the burned out cars along the way, destroyed by 50-

caliber machine gun fire, which remained testimony to previous attacks on military convoys. Threats still existed from the

occasional overpasses on the highway where insurgents would fire at the convoys. The more clever ones would tie a bomb to a string and throw it over the side of the overpass so it would detonate at a height just about where the gunners sat atop the Humvees. Alert convoy drivers countered by swerving wildly when traveling under the overpasses, trying to avoid any bombs from above. Our convoy swerved as it passed under the last underpass before Abu Ghraib prison. Now, the full view of the prison walls came into sight and seeing it for the first time I began nodding my head, impressed by its sheer size.

Abu Ghraib prison sits like a colossus on the western outskirts of Baghdad. A 20-foot concrete block wall completely surrounds the more than 250-acre complex. A perimeter several kilometers long with 15 towers manned by U.S.

soldiers and marines most often armed with 50-caliber machine guns, kept a watchful eye on the main roads bordering the complex. Guards accessed the tower at the base through a small metal door and climbed a ladder to the bird's nest lookout position, entering through a trap door in the floor. Once inside, the commanding view of the perimeter immediately dominated. Resourceful soldiers rigged a few armor barriers in strategic positions, defending against incoming small arms fire while preserving the line of fire for the heavy machine gun. Every so often a delivery truck or an errant taxi driver would test the system by exiting the highway at the prison, which is unauthorized. To the driver's surprise, he would be greeted with 50-caliber machine gun fire or a star cluster flare shot over the vehicle. If that didn't catch his attention the fire would be directed into the engine block, almost instantly stopping it in its tracks.

In several places along the perimeter, the town butted up against the wall and the cries from local mosques could be easily heard from most locations within. On occasion we could hear a rogue Imam preaching anti-Americanism to the faithful. In one place, an apartment complex sat less than 100 feet from the

wall but it had been cleared of dangerous types and an agreement with locals kept the flats inhabited by trusted citizens in exchange for allowing the apartments to remain so close to our facility.

Turning sharply from the highway onto a dirt road, several marines waved the vehicles through the checkpoint surrounded by cement obstacles known as Jersey barriers, and walls of huge metal framed sandbag-like containers known as Hesco barriers. Within a minute, all ten vehicles of our convoy were inside the relative safety of the compound and headed toward the dismount area. Colin was there to meet me as I exited the Humvee. "Welcome aboard," Colin smiled, shaking my hand while grabbing my heavy backpack with the other. "We have your quarters ready for you, so let's go straight over there before we get some chow."

Almost everyone assigned to Abu G lived in prison cells. It was actually the safest place in the prison. The thick cement walls and cement ceiling provided protection against mortar fire which the prison received almost everyday. With a few sheets of plywood and imagination, each person built a little privacy into the cells. Inside, each cell came equipped with a cot or maybe an old metal bunk bed. Mine had a few shelves made of cement blocks stacked several high with plywood stretched across to form a makeshift storage space. I threw my sleeping bag over the bare springs of the bottom bunk that would be home for the foreseeable future. I laid back and looked at the ceiling in disbelief that I had left my comfortable home for this. Noticing a thick metal hook hanging from the center of the cement ceiling, I thought, "Probably where Saddam hung prisoners and beat them as needed."

Inside the prison, which under Saddam reportedly contained 30,000 unfortunate souls, Americans and Iraqis held approximately 5,000 prisoners, in some cases the worst of the worst. Divided into two areas: Iraqi controlled and American controlled. The American area, known as Camp Redemption, guarded by U.S. Army military police (MP), consisted of five sections of tents surrounded by barbed wire. Each section housed prisoners of progressive importance. Section 1 housed the least important inmates and Section 5 housed the most dangerous. Almost central to the prison complex sat what was known as the Hard Site. This constituted a prison within a prison with separate walls and towers, guarded by Iraqi Correction Officers (ICO) who stood watch in the towers without weapons. If they saw someone try to escape I

suppose they could yell down to the Americans for help, but other than that they spent their tour of duty chatting with each other with little regard for their actual mission. Months later, the policy changed allowing one ICO in each tower to carry a shotgun but the truth was we could never completely trust the ICOs.

In one sense, I hated entering the Iraqi Hard Site, truly a wretched place. I detested the smell of body odor, urine, and raw human degradation. Filthy conditions, men crowded many to a small room, little or no running water, a hole in the floor to urinate; bluntly speaking the place stunk and exuded a kind of slime that irritated me. I learned to enter through the kitchen as there was far less security to overcome. It was quite ironic that to enter the Hard Site through the main entrance, you had to walk up to an iron gate within a long hallway. The hall actually had an iron gate at each end separated by about 100 feet. If no one on the inside expected you then the only way to gain entrance was to yell down to anyone, including prisoners that might walk by and motion that you needed to come in. That person would then yell for a guard to unlock the double gate system. In contrast, the back door of the kitchen, which led directly into the Hard Site, was almost always left open to receive deliveries and such. I learned to wind my way through the kitchen halls and storage rooms into the main cafeteria and out into the prison. This section of the prison was still cordoned off from most prisoners, but it allowed access to the main office area where the few Americans worked. Winding through those back halls was tricky as the floors retained a coat of slippery slime that would quickly send your feet out from under you if you did not walk lightly. It served as a constant reminder to me that I was entering the mini Iraqi world contained by the U.S. world surrounding it.

Within the Hard Site, multiple cellblocks, each two tiers high lined a long hallway down the middle of the building. A prisoner mafia ran the place with tier chiefs, cellblock chiefs, cell chiefs, etc. The ICOs were a joke. It was often difficult to tell the prisoners from the guards. No uniforms were required for the prisoners, little to no training for the Iraqi guards; in short, it was not professionally operated. A few U.S. advisors, American civilians with law enforcement or prison guard experience, advised the Iraqis. Generally professional, their hands were in many ways tied, preventing them from instituting the changes within the prison they knew were certainly needed. They often confided that the entire system required overhaul. Drugs and corruption were rampant. The Hard Site bore little resemblance to the operation of an American prison. You might say, "We have corruption, drugs, prison mafia and gangs in American prisons too." While correct, those problems in Iraqi prisons rise to a completely different level.

The corruption in Abu G meant that anything and everything could be had for a price. A defiant prisoner once told me that he could get anything he wanted in prison. We decided to test that claim challenging him to produce contraband. After a thorough body search and two nights in solitary confinement, at our next

22

meeting he proudly produced a pen with drugs concealed inside and a razor blade he kept hidden under his tongue for use as a weapon. Prisoners routinely purchased contraband items from the guards or from other prisoners. Contraband is always a problem in prisons and we worked hard to combat smuggling for a variety of reasons. First of all, by catching smugglers we learned the methods and identified troublesome personnel that often lead to uncovering larger problems. By detecting smuggled cigarettes and drugs we might learn how prisoners smuggled weapons, which of course is a major concern in any prison environment, but in a war zone prison housing insurgents and terrorists, the problem was amplified.

Weapons posed a particularly serious problem. At times we discovered not only knives and implements crafted to act as knives but also firearms, mostly crude handguns. Prisoners would conceal the weapons in hopes of building a cache that at the proper time could be used in a prison break, self defense situation, or just to kill Americans.

ICOs proved a major source of smuggling and they resorted to ingenious methods to penetrate the facility. All ICOs were subject to a thorough search by U.S. Marines at the Entry Control Point (ECP) before entering the prison grounds. Cigarettes functioned as currency in the prison so they had to be controlled. ICOs worked several days at a stretch and needed to bring in several packs at a time. Unfortunately, prisoners concealed drugs in the cigarettes by removing a portion of the tobacco and placing pills within. They became adept at fashioning the packs to appear sealed when in fact they had been tampered with. In response, we required ICOs to open packs so guards could squeeze individual cigarettes, feeling for contraband concealed within. Not to be deterred, ingenious ICOs took to smuggling drugs sewed into the lining of coats, forcing the Marines to check every coat thoroughly. Clever smugglers then switched to sewing them into the hems and borders of their shirts so we had to adjust again checking all those areas. Shoes served as another valuable smuggling device. Hollowed out heels were far too common and we discovered more than a few steel shanks or knife blades sewn into the soles. Belts of course provided a handy place to smuggle contraband and had to be removed and examined thoroughly. The hems and waistbands of pants posed similar difficulties. Trying to stay one step ahead of the smugglers required tremendous effort. By the time I left Abu G, the search process and partial disrobing of each person took an inordinate amount of time and still we were never fully able to curb the smuggling. All the while the ICOs complained that we didn't trust them and that such extensive searches violated their human rights.

Narcotics posed a second more dangerous problem. Besides the obvious degradation of good order and discipline, drugs contributed to the power of the prison mafia inside, which effectively used narcotics to control prisoners and activity within the facility. Those who could produce the contraband gained power within the hierarchy. But most dangerous to American military, the use of narcotics could induce a crazed state among prisoners hyping them up for an attack or a breakout. The majority of prisoners were desperate men to begin with, the drugs could put them over the top.

Catching prisoners with drugs sometimes yielded intelligence about how and from whom they obtained them, usually from another prisoner but the trail would eventually lead to a corrupt ICO. Interrogation of the ICO could then lead to connection on the outside, possibly to the insurgency.

From a CI perspective, however, the important commodity for prisoners was information, both that which might come into the prison as well as information sent out. Not all prisoners were die-hard loyal terrorists. The Hard Site held an odd mix of common criminals as well as insurgents. But even among those arrested for insurgent activity, some were merely superficially connected to the movement. For example, insurgents may target a poor unemployed man, offering him a few hundred dollars to plant an IED along the road one night. In the process he is caught and sent to prison. His crime was one of opportunity conducted without any devotion to the insurgency. In fact, he may not even know the identity of the insurgent that tasked him in the first place. This individual becomes a potential CI source if he can be tested and recruited properly. His insurgent status may provide access to comrades within the prison allowing him to report valuable information if he can learn the activities of the hard-core insurgents operating within. Let me paint a scenario where a man, I will call him Abdullah, might become valuable to the U.S. by becoming a mule for imprisoned insurgents.

Terrorists serving their sentence still need to communicate with the outside world. The network continues to function, in some ways more efficiently, within the prison where concentrations of insurgents spend a lot of time together. Imagine that insurgent Ahmed wants to receive and transmit messages to his supporters on the outside. Fearing discovery, he recruits Abdullah to mule messages through family contacts. In other words, Ahmed has his supporters contact Abdullah's wife or relatives and when the relatives visit Abdullah they carry messages for Ahmed. If CI agents can recruit Abdullah, then they can intercept those messages and possibly even learn the identity of the insurgents on the outside who contact Abdullah's relatives, through simple surveillance. Once identified, those insurgents can lead to other suspects and possibly caches of weapons, explosives, communication equipment or even kidnapped victims. Of course, the fact that Abdullah is cooperating with the U.S. must remain closely guarded not only for the safety of Abdullah but to ensure the information is never compromised. The net of insurgents that might ultimately be neutralized is more important than Abdullah or any one insurgent. Conversely, Ahmed will test Abdullah to be sure he is loyal and if his betrayal is discovered it would certainly cost Abdullah and his family their lives. In general, prisoners are far more afraid of other prisoners than the Americans. They know all too well the tentacles of the insurgency reach far into the community and not only could Abdullah be killed, but terrible things could happen to his wife or extended family. Naturally, Abdullah will resist cooperation with CI agents unless he sees a definite benefit to himself or his family and he can be convinced the CI agents can secure confidentiality. Finding the right person to act as an informant inside the prison requires hard work, the proper skill set, experience, and a bit of luck. Within the prison, jealousies and rivalries are the norm. Contrary to the old saying, there is little honor among thieves. Prisoners eagerly inform on each other to remove rivals or sometimes as retribution for someone who is abusing them sexually or physically, and both kinds of maltreatment are common in prison.

Outbound information is also critical. From the vantage point of the Hard Site, prisoners could see much of the prison complex. The insurgents mortared or even attacked Abu G regularly. In April 2005, insurgents mounted a coordinated attack on the prison from several angles. One prong engaged Marines manning a tower while another group attacked from a residential area near the wall. Using rocket propelled grenades, hand grenades and automatic weapons, the insurgents provided cover fire for a suicide car bomber trying to penetrate the south wall. The attack had caught the Marines off guard but they fought back fiercely, eventually killing fifty of the estimated sixty attackers, and directing heavy fire blowing up the suicide car bomber before he reached the wall. Thirty-six U.S. personnel sustained injuries.

Abu G suffered almost continuous insurgent threats. For one length of time, insurgents mortared the prison nearly every day. Inmates carefully noted where the mortars landed and tried to send messages to the insurgents about how close they had come to hitting key targets like command centers or barracks while insuring the rocketeers avoided areas housing detainees. Sending timely messages to the insurgency required mules that had access to the outside. That could include ICOs, other prison employees like doctors, staff and administration or visitors.

One might assume a maximum-security prison is a secure place, but security is relative. Any prison is only as secure as the people running it and the procedures used in operating the facility. Visitation posed a serious vulnerability for us. The identity of so-called family and friends visiting the prisoners was almost impossible to verify and no one really kept track of who came and how many times they visited. This information presented enormous CI potential at Abu Ghraib but U.S. intelligence exploited it poorly. Guards confided that senior level Iraqis, some believed connected to the insurgency, visited high ranking prisoners but no one seemed interested in exploiting the information. I estimated we missed dozens of chances to arrest insurgents that had boldly walked right into the prison as visitors because they felt safe that their true identity would not be discovered or even questioned.

The main entrance itself presented serious vulnerabilities. Everyday, hundreds of people—mostly women—crowded the gate hoping to gain entry to see their relatives, many just wanting to find out if their missing loved ones were actually inside. Unfortunately visitors could only enter by appointment. Potential visitors were required to come one day to apply for a visit and then receive an appointment to return another day. The average illiterate Iraqi, especially mothers and female relatives, knew nothing of the system and would crowd the gate hours before it opened pleading for help. It tugged at the heart to observe their passionate pleas, but it was impossible to help them for lack of translators or other personnel. It would take an entire day or longer to answer all their questions. Some posed impossible questions such as, "Is my son Mohamed here?" or "Please check for my cousin Ahmed, he is *this* tall with black hair."

Complicating matters even more was the startling fact that Iraqi prison officials did not know exactly who was in custody. I could not believe it when I first discovered this tragedy. I was shocked. I remember interviewing an inmate inside the prison who provided information about another prisoner allegedly connected to the insurgency. I will call the source of the information Kasim.

Having no history with Kasim, I tried to verify every detail he passed to me. The most important thing Kasim said during one session was that another prisoner, I will call him Mohammed Yasir, actively communicated with the insurgency from inside the prison. He told me that Mohammed lived in Cellblock H and the actual cell number. Eager to test the reliability of Kasim, I visited Iraqi prison authorities and asked them to verify if Mohammed Yasir lived in the cellblock as stated by Kasim. After reviewing their antiquated paper filing system, the officials announced there was no such person in the prison. Slightly perturbed that the inmate had duped me I insisted the administrator check several times, always producing the same result. I scheduled a meeting the following day with Kasim prepared to unload on him for lying to me.

Eventually confronting him about Mohammed not being in the prison, Kasim looked at me oddly, cocking his head slightly and squinting his eyes as if I were crazy. He insisted that Mohammed lived exactly where he said the day before and encouraged me to go check for myself. Sensing his sincerity, I concocted a ruse where the interpreter and an Iraqi ICO would visit the cellblock and ask for several persons including Mohammed. To my surprise, just as Kasim had said, Mohammed was there. Now, even more confounded I approached the American advisors and told them the story. Unphased by my revelation, they confided that the Iraqi authorities only really kept an accurate count of about 40% of the prisoners. The others no one really knew for sure. Determined to run this to its end, I returned to the Iraqi administration office and explained the entire situation. A young Iraqi official shrugged his shoulders and nonchalantly replied that people came and went from the prison all the time, some were transferred, others left for trial and may not have returned. Without emotion he confirmed that the prison records were spotty at best and the 40% number quoted by the advisors was as good as any. He seemed genuinely unconcerned that prison authorities did not know exactly who was detained there. I was dumbfounded. I could not believe a prison could operate this way but it was the reality and the environment we were forced to work within.

Red Cross Visit

I will never forget the first time I experienced an International Red Cross visit. The team members were so politically liberal and anti-military they seemed determined to stir trouble. I couldn't gain access to the briefing room for their in-brief with the Commanding General but my colleagues told me about the comedy that unfolded inside.

The first words spoken by the team chief to the U.S. General and his staff during the in-brief were, "All these prisoners are part of an illegal war and are here illegally, they should be released immediately." To the General's credit he simply ignored the request replying, "Next issue." Then they began with the complaint, "The prisoners do not have enough hot water." The General impatiently countered, "My soldiers do not have enough hot water, next issue." And so the briefing went item after item.

Later, I ran into one of the International Red Cross representatives walking around the base. She came from Switzerland and I struck up a conversation with her. Almost immediately she commented that the conditions were deplorable in

Abu G. I asked where else she had inspected and she mentioned Cambodia and Vietnam. Inquiring where the conditions were better she admitted they were better at Abu Ghraib but she said, "We should expect the conditions to be worse in Vietnam." She was so quick to condemn our running of the prison but would not condemn the Cambodians or the Vietnamese no matter what abuses or conditions she observed elsewhere. I found the entire exchange difficult to believe or tolerate.

I wonder how she would have responded to the September 2006, UK Telegraph report of how prisoners reacted when Americans turned over Abu Ghraib to Iraqi authorities. One prisoner was quoted as saying, "The Americans were better than the Iraqis. They treated us better." Another reportedly shouted, "Please help us, we want the human rights officers, we want the Americans to come back." A third, Haleem Aleulami who had been released from jail said, "The Americans had treated him better when they ran the jail."[1] Somehow those stories don't make it far in the U.S. press, or into her background notes.

---

[1] Saber, Ali and Gethin Chamberlain. "Tortured screams ring out as Iraqis take over Abu Ghraib." Telegraph. 11 Sept. 2006. 21 July 2008 <http://www.telegraph.co.uk/news/1528513/Tortured-screams-ring-out-as-Iraqis-take-over-Abu-Ghraib.html>.

3   Our Iraqi Hosts

Two mosques were located near enough to our perimeter walls that we could hear the prayers broadcast from the beautiful minarets into the community over loudspeakers, five times per day. Occasionally, I would climb into one of the towers and observe life around a nearby mosque. Our military convoys frequently traveled the thoroughfare passing in front of the mosque and I could see quite a way down that road from my vantage point in the tower. With the naked eye, I could observe the very spot where the night before, a daisy chain IED went off as one of our convoys returned from patrol. An IED, a military acronym for "improvised explosive device" is usually buried along the road and remotely detonated when a vehicle passes by. The daisy chain is a group of IEDs set to explode as a convoy passes, thus ensuring the chance of damaging multiple vehicles. It sounds like someone lit a pack of firecrackers when the explosions start popping everywhere. I had not heard yet if the unit had suffered any casualties in that incident but just before we arrived in the tower, an IED exploded along the road near the mosque. No one was injured but one of our vehicles sustained damage. I scanned the streets for any sign of suspicious persons but detected no one. A few people walked along both sides, some entering and exiting local stores. One of the tower guards told me he had shot a man pointing a machine gun along that road once before. "Nice shot," I thought as it looked pretty far to me, more than several hundred yards.

Every Friday, we took special notice of the services at the mosques and the commentary broadcast over the loudspeakers into the streets. Usually, the local Imam read the Quran for about 20 minutes and then said a few words, a kind of sermon. I could not help think, "Just imagine if Christians tried this back home, it would certainly rouse complaints and calls of separation of church and state." Anyway, some citizens listened, others went about their business, but life at least slowed down during that period. My impression was that the people were quite poor and simple. It was hard to imagine their rugged faces and the difficult lives they lead. Our cultures were so different and yet there were similarities. They loved their families, especially children, like we did. Their lives centered around their faith in God, except theirs was outward and visible, not easily avoided under the watchful eyes of others. Our faith is private and personal, easily disregarded as we go about making a living, focused on individual success, and distracted from our faith by the cares of the world. Our society is based on the rule of law, theirs on ancient customs and the word of the Holy Quran, which most of our young men and women serving in Iraq know almost nothing about. To them we look like decadent, evil people, addicted to sex, pornography and the trappings of materialism. To

34

the devout among them we are stuck in *Jahiliyah*, meaning ignorant of divine guidance. We are a society of "hooking up," binge drinking, rampant internet porn, sexualization of women, homosexuality, secularization, consumerism and general ignorance of the Holy Book we claim to follow. They see themselves as knowledgeable of the word of God spoken in the Quran, which a large number have memorized since childhood; they try to follow his word but are oppressed by the evil influences in the world, mainly the U.S., spreading its perverted influences and sex obsessed culture to Muslim lands. They see themselves as the liberators of oppressed people, freeing them to serve God, not materialism. To us they look like fanatics stuck in a backward civilization inferior to our own. We see ourselves as protectors of freedom, liberators of an oppressive system which crushes individual rights, champions of personal liberty and the freedom to worship God in your own way or not to worship at all. Bridging the gap is difficult and slow, and progressing at a pace of one person at a time.

Quite a few of the workers inside the prison were Iraqi Christians or other outcasts from the society under Saddam. One man had been captive in Abu Ghraib prison under Saddam for merely appearing to speak against the regime. He had suffered horrible beatings and torture within the prison which was crowded with five times the number that were presently incarcerated. He told gruesome stories of what happened to other prisoners he knew during that period. Another middle-aged man told me of his arrest under the Saddam regime because he had voted "no" on the ballot, against Saddam. Officials later "corrected" the obvious error. I remember a bright 25-year old man with a 5th grade education who had worked as a busboy since childhood. It was the only thing he knew and all he had to look forward to the rest of his life. As a practicing Christian he had suffered much persecution even under Saddam. Life under Saddam was tough for the average citizen not part of the ruling elite. Another man confided how he had spent 12 years as a POW in Iran during the Iran-Iraq war. When he returned, Saddam gave him a $25 reward. He hated Saddam. Most Iraqis suffered 30 years of terror under the madman, especially Kurds and Christians. In southern and northeastern Iraq, Saddam is hated universally.

On New Years Eve we worked all day, there were no real holidays in Iraq for the U.S. military. Some areas tried to celebrate in a fashion but the war did not stop for American holidays. That day, several Iraqis waiting at the gate were reportedly threatened by insurgents. Most of our workers lived in town. If insurgent informants recognized they worked in the prison, the employees or their families could suffer threats, injury, or even death. Others were approached to work for the insurgents gathering intelligence about what went on inside the prison. They may want to know the security arrangements, access procedures, names of people working inside, a variety of information insurgents might use as leverage in recruiting sources inside the prison. Al Qaeda worked tirelessly to

36

infiltrate Abu G as it did most U.S. military installations. A year later, the press reported that Al-Qaeda's plan to infiltrate security guards in Baghdad had been foiled by the Iraqi Interior Ministry, which didn't surprise me since we had battled insurgents trying to infiltrate Abu G at every opportunity.

We documented the information given by the ones threatened that day but such incidents were fairly common. A few claimed they had been approached in the parking lot by a man in a vehicle warning them that they worked for the Americans at their peril unless they switched loyalties to the insurgency. Documenting as much of a description as possible we often passed it to the Quick Reaction Force (QRF) to be on the lookout for Arabs matching the description and roll them up, military jargon for arrest them. Once arrested, we would have a crack at interviewing them. QRF soldiers patrolled the parking lot which sat several hundred yards from the visitor's gate. It also patrolled the road along that side of the perimeter.

Detainees rolled up on patrol routinely were processed through the IHA (Interrogation Holding Area), where MPs strip searched them, gave them a prison outfit, medically examined them, and provided them a meal, usually an MRE (Meals Ready to Eat), if the detainee wanted one. The base commander had 72 hours to sort out whether the allegations against the detainees contained merit. If warranted, suspects would be processed for formal detention in the prison. If not, they could be released.

Once administratively processed into the prison they became subject to an odd judicial procedure explained to me by the Army Magistrate. Two judicial tracks existed for prisoners: prosecution or a Board of Decision. If the U.S. military wished to prosecute in Iraqi court the military must provide statements from two witnesses and produce pictures if the incident involved an IED or cache of weapons. "No pictures, no conviction," the Major explained curtly. An Iraqi judge reviewed the case and a three-judge panel decided guilt or innocence. Individual cases could take as little as 15 minutes. The second course usually involved individuals designated "of intelligence interest."[2] These people could be kept in prison for six months before their case must be

---

[2] For example, while interviewing a person for planting an IED we discover he had traveled to Afghanistan a year earlier to an Al Qaeda training camp. Obviously, he now becomes of intelligence interest because he possesses strategic information that will take time to draw out and document. Interrogators will try to ascertain further information such as how he was selected for the training, how he made his way to Afghanistan, which countries he traveled through, who assisted him, what travel documents were used, were any documents forged, how and where did he obtain them, can he identify any persons attending training at the same time, can he identify persons working at the camp, can he describe the training curriculum, what weapons did he learn to use, what bomb making techniques, and who taught them? All this and much more is strategic information that is beyond the perishable tactical information concerning potentially lethal IEDs needed to be captured in the initial interviews at the ground level. Strategic information can take months to acquire and may lead to other lines of questioning developed from the detainee's answers.

presented to a board consisting of three U.S. military members and four Iraqis. If the board decided the person was guilty or of intelligence interest he could be held in the prison for another six months when his case would be reviewed again. This process could repeat indefinitely, effectively resulting in a possible life sentence, six months at a time.

CI agents received the first shot at detainees arrested on patrol. Several times a day we would be called to interview the detainees and help sort out the allegations by corroborating their story or obtaining a confession. I discovered a genuine problem with using Marines and Army infantry in law enforcement situations as they were not trained for this mission and, although they did the best they could, innocent people were frequently rolled up along with legitimate insurgents.

I recall the time that while out on patrol Marines spotted a man squatting along the road beside his car. According to the short written report of only two paragraphs, it looked like the Iraqi was digging a hole to plant an IED. The Marines turned their vehicle around to investigate further and the suspect jumped in his car and fled the scene. They quickly apprehended the suspect for suspicion of planting IEDs. In fact, that area had been a hotbed of IEDs in the past so the Marines were understandably edgy, given the very real threat out there and the fact that it was their lives on the line every time they stepped out into the city. However, as I stated, once a prisoner is apprehended the process for him to appear before a

Magistrate and be released can take up to six months if for whatever reason, the CI agents don't receive the case, or otherwise conclude it favorably within the 72 hour period. The cases were so numerous that not every one could be investigated in 72 hours. If an innocent man spends six months waiting for justice, then the U.S. has severely disrupted his life and most likely made an enemy of him. Obviously, we tried our best to resolve these issues quickly.

This particular suspect was taken to the IHA and we received the call. Always anxious to interview IED planters, I hustled over to the IHA to talk to him. At first he said he did nothing and had no idea why he had been picked up by the patrol. Within an hour the man admitted he had stopped to take a crap along the road and was trying to cover it up with dirt. He swore by Allah of his innocence and offered to show us the exact spot of the steamy pile he left behind. In tears, the suspect claimed he ran away because he knew that to be detained for any reason could result in a long wait in prison and he had old, sick parents to care for, an excuse routinely given but unfortunately too often, at least partially true. After talking with the Marines and radioing for the patrol to check out the story, we determined the suspect was in fact telling the truth. No one faulted the Marines as a reasonable person would have been suspicious of the man's actions but with a little more discernment at the scene we might have prevented him and other innocents from being detained. We all wanted to catch the "bad guys" but we DID NOT want to catch GOOD GUYS. All of us who participated in the case had a good laugh at a suspect rolled up for crapping along the road but it was indicative of the larger problem resulting from using infantry in law enforcement. The issue is a sticky one. Soldiers and Marines were supposedly given rudimentary law enforcement training but the truth was that when they could not distinguish good guys from bad, they apprehended everyone in the area. Our soldiers and Marines must be allowed to protect themselves but I felt confident that if we provided more training on apprehension and simple crime scene information gathering, we could clear more innocents and concentrate on the real insurgents. I was certain we could improve the process but the issue proved too macro for the military to show concern at the time. Americans are compassionate and fair-minded people, but given the circumstances, my perception of the overall attitude toward this issue was "we will do what we can." War fighting understandably remained the number one priority. If a few Iraqis spent some unnecessary time in jail that was the cost of war. Again, I acknowledge that in time of war the system will never be perfect, but with additional law enforcement training and coaching by CI agents, we could have reduced law enforcement related problems. This presented another challenge I will discuss later, that in the U.S. Army, CI agents are not trained or experienced in law enforcement.

The pace slowed as the day wore on. Other than dodging the daily mortar attacks, the Marines decided to conduct an unannounced check of all foreigners leaving the compound.

Unexpectedly the guards discovered a vanload of Iraqis leaving the post with an air conditioner and other government equipment hidden in the back. Six Iraqis, who ran the hadji laundry on post, crowded the van to its limits. GIs had a habit of calling everything Iraqi hadji. I do not know the origin but they used it in the pejorative, meaning poorly built, poorly done or just poor. On base we had both a military laundry and a hadji laundry. KBR (Kellogg Brown and Root), a U.S. military contractor, ran the military laundry which offered a two day service to soldiers. It took longer because the clothes were actually sent to Baghdad for cleaning. Unfortunately, sometimes KBR (Kellogg Brown and Root) employees lost entire bags of clothes or at least part of the batch you turned in. The hadji laundry provided same day or next day service performed right on post. The military laundry was free; the hadji laundry cost $6.00 a load. A sizable number of soldiers preferred the hadji laundry allowing the Iraqis to develop a thriving business on base. In general, military customers liked the hadji workers and when we shut down their laundry to investigate the possible air conditioner theft, people complained almost immediately. I had to rebuke several U.S. friends of the hadji who pleaded for their release claiming, "There must be some mistake," or "the hadji could not have possibly stolen anything." I spent all day and into the night interviewing them. They consistently denied all allegations, adamant they were taking the air conditioner (and other equipment) into town to be repaired. All six provided almost the same exact

42

statements. Minimal investigation revealed their rehearsed story was certainly a lie because KBR serviced all the air conditioners on post so there was no need to take it into town. In fact, KBR records confirmed the air conditioning unit had been serviced only weeks before. Finally, several of them confessed to stealing it to sell in the Baghdad market.

Stealing air conditioners in itself had little CI connection. My deeper concern was that these guys had access to the base and traveled daily into Baghdad, making them valuable recruitment targets for the insurgency. Their access not only to the base but to hundreds of military personnel who befriended them, made these six Iraqis of definite CI interest. In addition, what I learned from several of the workers during the interview caught my attention. It seemed the owner of the laundry was a mysterious Iraqi that never came to the prison but operated hadji laundries on several U.S. military installations throughout Iraq. Intelligence we collected gave us added reason to believe he maintained connections to the insurgency or at least paid them protection money. This obviously merited further inquiry. Meanwhile, without my knowledge, the Base Commander exercised his prerogative to summon the manager of the hadji laundry and read him the riot act before giving him another chance and allowing him to return to work. I protested that my report clearly documented the evidence and their confessions, in addition to the suspicions concerning the owner. Our Base Commander was what soldiers like to call a kick-ass guy. Tall and imposing, he was all soldier and no nonsense. I respected him immensely, especially his dedication to securing that prison and protecting his troops. I presented my case to him personally. He listened intently then explained that he believed the manager was sufficiently frightened enough and the closure of the laundry was too severe a morale problem. He wanted that laundry opened ASAP. I understood the Commander's concern for morale but I felt the workers should have been further investigated as a CI threat. At the very least they should have been fired and blacklisted from all U.S. military posts. The Commander disagreed and he possessed the final authority. The Iraqis stayed but the Commander told me to keep an eye on them and if they slipped up again he would throw them in the prison. Without a doubt, he had more pressing issues on his mind that day. At our afternoon staff meeting the S-2 representative, Hiram Dahmer, briefed that insurgents fired four mortars at the camp and an IED caused one U.S. casualty to one of our convoys entering the compound. I suppose the Commander was thinking more of active threats than potential threats. But the example further confirmed for me a systemic misunderstanding of CI in the U.S. Army. I felt in general that Army Commanders either did not value their CI assets or lacked a full appreciation of how we could help them neutralize insurgent threats to installations. But that was an issue transcending Abu G.

Keeping an eye on laundry workers did not constitute the most productive use of time when we had captured insurgents to interview daily. Beyond that my mind was continually occupied by how to protect the base in general. Defending this compound seemed much like protecting an Air Force base, a task I had plenty of experience performing. Normally, we could recruit local sources in rings around the base, extending out as far as several miles to inform us of trouble long before insurgents could reach the base. Locals could alert us to strangers observing or even asking suspicious questions, anything out of the ordinary. The problem remained we were not allowed to function outside the wire and were prohibited from tasking sources, even those who worked inside the base. Our area (the prison) was run by the U.S. Army and was situated on the border of the 1ˢᵗ Cavalry Division territory.[3] Villages just outside our camp were the responsibility of the Marine 5ᵗʰ MEF in Fallujah. The Marines were authorized to run sources outside our camp but the prison sat on the edge of their area of responsibility (AOR) and they were always spread too thin to effectively care about a place so far out. Besides, they assumed the Army would take care of it. The main concern of the Marines at that time was Fallujah, not Abu Ghraib. It became a catch-22 that hindered our ability to gather intelligence that might protect us. Given authority

---

[3] 1ˢᵗ Cavalry Division was later replaced after normal troop rotation.

45

to task local national sources, they could have warned us of IEDs along the road and alerted us to pending mortar attacks, among other vital CI information. But the bureaucracy defeated us again and the turf squabble prevented us from perfecting our mission accomplishment. Not that the Marines did not want to help, they were always dedicated and we worked well together, but there were too few of them and they could only do so much. This type of bureaucratic snafu was common in the military environment. Fighting it proved a waste of time and in the grand scheme of things, one just had bigger battles to attend.

I awoke again to morning prayers blaring from the two local mosques around 5:00 am. I struggled to understand our hosts. The Muslims appeared devoted to God with their praying five times per day. Even the prisoners stopped to pray. This happened to be the month of the *Haj*, the pilgrimage to Mecca that all Muslims must make at least once in their lives. It stands in importance as one of the five pillars of Islam. Thousands of Muslims would pass through Iraq to reach Mecca in Saudi Arabia. In honor of Islam, the Iraqi government opened the border to pilgrims. Of course, this meant that fresh insurgents would also enter the country under the guise of pilgrims. The timing could not have been worse since the first Iraqi elections were scheduled the same month and insurgents were increasing their ferocity in order to disrupt the elections. At the time, we did not know their efforts would prove unsuccessful, largely due to the massive security effort of U.S. and Iraqi forces.

Back inside the prison, I was proud to have cleared an innocent man this day. Marines arrested an Iraqi ICO at the gate that morning carrying unidentified drugs and a syringe. Sharp-eyed Marine guards found the material as the ICO tried to leave the base. My subsequent investigation revealed he was actually telling the truth. The frightened ICO claimed the drugs were prescribed by the prison doctor. I visited the prison doctor inside the Hard Site. For me it proved another wretched visit into that facility. As I approached his office it looked like chaos. Out in the hall, prisoners lined up with no guards in sight. Inside, a technician helped with administration but the doctor worked tirelessly and appeared overwhelmed by the long lines of prisoners waiting for examination. One interesting thing about the prisoners is they all were concerned about their health and a large number seemed afflicted with high blood pressure. Generally, their health was relatively poor. Once I interviewed a man who looked in his 50s. His date of birth was listed as 1974. When I questioned if it was a mistake, the man almost cried, explaining he had lived a hard life. I did not mean to hurt his feelings but he admitted that people often guessed he was much older. This is typical for citizens of the third world. Their health is so poor, with a large number overweight, and what they eat is not good for them, often fat and greasy (sounds like our situation in the U.S.). Anyway, as I cut to the head of the line to see the doctor, the prisoners all looked at me, at once frightened and curious. There was almost no privacy in the prison and the doctor insisted he was too busy to step outside for an interview. He admitted prescribing the medicine for the ICO. I also learned that it was not unusual to issue syringes to patients as Iraqis commonly injected themselves with medicine. The doctor did not understand my interest in the man's medicine. I tried to explain that drugs in the prison were considered a serious security matter. He gave an odd glance, barely looking away from his patients, "Look around, what do these men have to look forward to?"

A misunderstanding between the Hard Site prison officials and the U.S. military caused the arrest. It would have been proper for the Iraqi doctor to write the ICO a letter authorizing him to carry the drugs through the post. However, the Iraqis didn't see the need. I suggested that we create a mandatory procedure to address this in the future but as did many ideas, it soon fell through the cracks. In the meantime, this innocent guy would have spent at least a few nights in jail had we not quickly resolved the issue. If he had spent time in custody an otherwise pro-American guard might have turned against us for treating him unfairly. Instead, he was grateful that we resolved the matter quickly, allowing him to return home without spending even one night in the IHA. As I explained before, the number of trustworthy ICOs was so small I did not want to lose one that might be somewhat honest. In addition, since I had saved this officer considerable heartache he was now obligated to me and potentially could be recruited to provide valuable information in the future. In several respects it was easier to recruit an ICO than a prisoner because the ICO had more to lose and would cooperate to keep his job. Prisoners had less to gain and could be killed by fellow prisoners if their cooperation was discovered.

As we drew closer to Iraq's first election the insurgents tried to increase disruptive activities. I recall one news account:

BAGHDAD (Reuters - January 4, 2005) – Gunmen killed Baghdad's governor in Iraq's highest-profile assassination in eight months and a suicide bomber killed 11 people at a police checkpoint on Tuesday in an escalating campaign to wreck the Jan. 30 election.

The shooting of Governor Ali al-Haidri in a roadside ambush showed insurgents' power to strike at the heart of the governing class, raising fresh doubts as to whether security forces can protect politicians and voters as the ballot draws near.

A group led by Al Qaeda ally Abu Musab al-Zarqawi, behind most of the bloodiest attacks since the U.S.-led invasion in 2003, claimed responsibility for the assassination, saying its fighters had struck down a "tyrant and American agent." The group said it was also behind the suicide bombing.

Insurgents also killed three U.S. soldiers in a roadside bomb attack in Baghdad; another soldier in

49

a bomb blast in Balad north of the capital; and an
American Marine in western Iraq.

We stayed busy as there were always suspects to interview
in the IHA. On this day I interviewed an Iraqi Arab in his late
twenties apprehended by the Marines for planting an IED on MSR
(Main Supply Route) Michigan days before on Christmas Day. He
detonated it as a U.S. convoy passed by and quickly escaped. A
little more than a week later he returned to the scene and luckily a
few Marines recognized him. The Marines quickly arrested him and
put him directly into the prison before I knew he was here. Usually,
I received notice that a prisoner was on the way in and allowed the
full 72 hours to interview the suspect before they processed him into
the prison. I had him pulled out and interrogated him with a young
Marine from the HET (Human Exploitation Team). After hours of
questioning the prisoner stuck to his story of innocence. We entered
Camp Redemption to search his personal property. He had been
placed in one of the scores of tents.

As I waited for the MPs to empty the tent of the other
prisoners, I decided to look around a bit. The military divided the
inmates into five levels. Level five was where the hard-core
terrorists and crazies were kept. My man stayed in level two. As I
turned around I noticed a cage with what looked like a lump under a
blanket. Slowly, the front of the blanket lifted to reveal two
yellowish eyes peering out from the darkness inside. It was an eerie

feeling. The man looked straight into my eyes. We stared at each other for some time before he once again slowly disappeared below the blanket. An MP saw our exchange of stares and told me the prisoner had been a "bad boy," unruly, spitting at guards and fighting with the other prisoners so they had placed him in solitary confinement. I began thinking how to approach this individual sometime in the future. An Army sergeant interrupted my thought asking if I could help him out by looking over a few documents in Arabic his men had seized from prisoners. Some of the notes were taken directly from prisoners, others were seized when prisoners tried passing them from one level to the next. Prisoners routinely tied notes to rocks and threw them over the fence from one level to one other, a crude but often effective message system. Alert guards frequently intercepted the messages but had no one to read them. I asked if they sent them up through Military Intelligence (MI) for exploitation and the MP responded that MI was not interested, claiming they were tied up with more important tasks. The MPs had rare interpreter support so the notes just piled up. My interpreter looked through a few of them and didn't notice anything alarming but he was not an intelligence officer. I wanted to translate them and look at the text personally but we were already busy. I promised the sergeant that our unit would help as much as possible in the future. We took a few notes with us for later examination.

By now all the prisoners, about twenty, had been removed from the tent. The MPs brought out our suspect's belongings, a few pieces of clothes, a blanket, and a few odds and ends. Donning rubber gloves we began to search the items, checking every article thoroughly for any incriminating evidence he might have concealed, but found nothing of value. We returned to the IHA and worked on the suspect into the night. The Marine interrogator and myself were determined to elicit a confession or develop evidence that would help send this guy to prison. In time, through patient questioning, we identified inconsistencies in his story that eventually caused his entire alibi to fall apart. It looked like one more IED planter would be off the streets for a while.

What I thought would be a quiet Sunday quickly gained excitement. A level five prisoner escaped early that morning. By the time I reached my office the entire prison was in lock down. Of course you might imagine a prison is always in lock down but in reality it isn't. The inside of the containment areas are secured but the 250-acre complex bustles with soldiers both on and off duty walking to the dining facility or to the recreation center, gym, barber shop, the post exchange or even the hadji shops run by locals. In addition, contractors and maintenance personnel are about. Hundreds of people can be seen traveling to and fro within the compound at any given time. When lockdown is in effect, military personnel are placed at key locations within the compound to check everyone's identification. That morning the entire post remained on the lookout for the prisoner and his freedom was short lived. By 0830 hrs, the MPs had recaptured him, an embarrassment rectified.

4   TRANSLATORS

Most of our local national translators (called terps) were either Christian (the majority) or non-practicing Muslims. They were happy to work with us for they had suffered persecution under Saddam. Now they enjoyed freedom. Some of the translators were raised under Islam but were nominal Muslims. As a rule, local national translators are only assigned to non-sensitive jobs such as work crews or hospital duty. Intelligence and CI terps possessed a higher classification known as Category 1 OSD (Office of Secretary of Defense), Category 2, or Category 3. Cat 1 OSD translators were recruited mainly from the U.S. but also from other allied countries including Canada or England. Their distinction—although they had lived in a Western country for a length of time, they had not yet acquired citizenship. In general, interpreters had no experience translating. They were merely average citizens who spoke Arabic and English. Titan Corporation, the company awarded the contract to provide interpreters, could not fill all the vacancies despite the more than six figure salaries paid to some interpreters. Because of the shortage it seemed just about anyone willing to serve in Iraq was recruited. Quite a few had bad attitudes, questionable English language ability and a host of other personal and professional problems.

One of the most famous cases involved Ahmed F. Melhalba. Born in Egypt, he emigrated to the U.S. eventually becoming a naturalized American citizen. He joined the Army wanting to become a CI agent but failed the course and eventually accepted a medical discharge from the service. Titan hired him as an Arabic linguist and sent him to Guantanamo Bay. He was arrested in 2003, after returning from Egypt carrying classified material and making false statements to FBI agents. Later sentenced to 20 months in prison, he was released in 2005.[4] The New York Times reported that, "Despite his discharge, Mr. Mehalba was able to get a job as translator for the military, through a contractor, the Titan Corporation of San Diego. Ralph Williams, a spokesman for Titan, said the company was not responsible for checking and certifying Mr. Melhalba's background."[5] As I will show throughout this book, my experience with government

---

[4] United States District Court, District of Massachusetts, Criminal Complaint, US v Ahmed Fathy Mehalba. 29 Sept. 2003.

[5] Lewis, Neil A., "Guantanamo Inquiry Widens as Civilian Translator is held." New York Times. 1 Oct. 2003. 23 July 2008 <http://query.nytimes.com/gst/fullpage.html?res=9A00E3D91F3DF93 2A35753C1A9659C8B63>.

contractors was similar. In general, they did not check employee backgrounds well and were more concerned about filling slots with warm bodies than providing quality employees to the U.S. military. In my opinion, this resulted in chronic problems of dishonesty and vulnerability to infiltration of the insurgency. Failing to thoroughly check backgrounds before hire and lack of verification after employment contributed to criminal activity and extortion, which could be used for personal gain or even worse, could aid the insurgent cause, an example of which is discussed below.

Other terps learned fast and became quite proficient. During my year in Iraq, I had the pleasure of working with some really fine terps but too many that should never have been hired in the first place. I met some real characters among the terps in Baghdad. One young man, Sammy, came from Chicago, although he had been born in Baghdad and was not a U.S. citizen yet. A pleasant man, Sammy became friends with just about everyone he met. He spoke with a kind of street savvy that I liked and was one of the few capable terps I briefly worked with in Baghdad. Cat 2 interpreters possessed U.S. citizenship and had passed a background investigation necessary to carry a security clearance up to the secret level. Cat 3 interpreters, few and far between, had to pass a more stringent background check and were authorized access up to top-secret information. The pay increased significantly for these interpreters. I was told a Cat 1 OSD interpreter could earn $80-90,000 a year or more depending on how long they stayed in country. Each category above that could expect a raise of $20,000 to 30,000 per year. To provide context to the cost of translators in Iraq, the World Tribune reported in February 2008 that the latest contract for translators scheduled through 2013 could cost U.S. taxpayers $4.6 billion, that's billion with a "B."[6] I imagine the first five years cost a similar amount, in my opinion mostly wasted money. These contractors were highly paid and some had not even earned a college education. What they had was language ability in high demand. The young soldiers they translated for earned only a fraction of their salary and often resented the high salaries paid to the terps. But the salaries were a result of supply and demand and Arabic terps remained in high demand and short supply throughout my tour in Iraq.

At the prison, a number of terps worked in the interrogation center. One gentleman assigned to the S-2 intelligence staff was shared by our unit. He was a likable enough older man, I will call Ali, but had major difficulty in that he resisted direction and considered himself an intelligence officer. After translating for intelligence organizations or CI agents for a year or two, terps

---

[6] "U.S. tab for translation services in Iraq could hit $4.6 billion." WorldTribune.com. 22 Feb. 2008. 21 July 2008 <http://www.worldtribune.com/worldtribune/WTARC/2008/ss_iraq_0 2_22.asp>.

56

sometimes began to think they understood counterintelligence better than the actual agents. In one sense it was understandable since the Army often sent young CI agents to the field. In Arab culture, a fifty-something year old man, college educated and able to speak several languages can feel insulted working under the direction of a 21-year-old high school educated Sergeant with a few months training in CI. This presented a number of operational problems. When a terp decides he knows what is important he begins to selectively translate the conversation. Such behavior can lead to dangerous results. The interrogator can miss critical clues that might save lives or the terp may assume power that can foster a corrupting influence. Since they are the only ones who really know what is being said it is hard to catch them. A savvy investigator will test his terp at intervals to ensure he is not going astray, but far too many of the young CI agents become enamored with the terps, allowing them to guide their actions.

In our unit, with the shortage of interpreters, we had use of the commander's terp too. Candice came from Lebanon with a very high opinion of herself. She was nice enough but very particular about her status and testy when it came to working with men. Her fear of being identified by terrorists compounded matters. Although she agreed to enter the Hard Site, she was extremely reluctant and worried the entire time, with good reason. Candice and other female terps she knew had been threatened by insurgents. It can be difficult for Muslim females to work in such an environment, but our translator was Christian. Even so, she had to overcome the attitudes of Muslim men who had different ideas of the proper role of women. A few refused to talk with a female present, others showed complete indifference. I tried to use the Lebanese female as much as possible because I distrusted Ali.

A more strategic problem for intelligence professionals involved the English translation of names. There are multiple derivations of Arabic names. Mohammed for example can be spelled Mahamed, Mahemmed, Mohamid, Muhammed, etc. If entered into a database we might not hit on an individual with a prior record because the name was input with a slightly different spelling. I remembered a very similar problem in the Orient with Chinese names but there we utilized the Chinese Telegraphic Code (CTC) for all Chinese names. The CTC reduced the complicated Chinese characters to numbers removing all doubt as to the exact name. I desperately wanted to develop an Arabic form of this code while in Iraq but could find no support for it. Everyone was too focused on micro issues to attack such a macro problem.

Another far more simple issue befuddled young troops and even some of the terps, the naming system of the Arabs. Typically when you encounter a name like Mohammed Yousif Abrahim what you are looking at is the individual's first name, his father's first name and his grandfather's first name, a system much different to what Westerners are used to. It became confusing for Americans to recognize how Ali Mohammed Yousif could be the son of

Mohammed Yousif Abrahim. Quite a few soldiers just threw up their hands and let the terps figure it out. Cultural differences such as these proved important in CI and I strongly maintained that all soldiers should have received better cultural training beyond the one-hour block during in-processing. Our ignorance of this very foreign culture often reduced our operational effectiveness.

5   Prison Informants

Every CI agent worth his salt knows that making oneself available can lead to developing solid information through sources. Regularly interviewing prisoners helped me develop a reputation as a person willing to listen, keep his promises, protect informants and act on critical intelligence. Admittedly, prisoners can take advantage of an agent to help eliminate rivals or enemies, by revealing information about them. Such motives are acceptable to us since our main effort is to catch "bad guys." Simply put, if one bad guy tells on another, it's fine with me. It is even encouraged— as long as it can be verified. On one occasion a prisoner from the Hard Site sent a message through prison advisors, asking to see me.

A Shiite, confined among mostly Sunnis, he had enemies without doubt. Tall with a full black beard he possessed a gentle demeanor. Standing in his orange prison jumpsuit with his white and black checkered yashmag (the colorful headscarf worn by Iraqis) wrapped neatly over his head, we surveyed each other before saying a word. He was familiar with me due to my frequent visits to the prison but I didn't know him well. As we got to know each other, I learned Ahmed was clever, always careful with his words, cautiously watching my reaction after speaking. He warmed to me almost immediately, talking about his life and his religion, fitting nicely my profile of someone potentially recruitable. A false notion persists in some intelligence circles that blond, blue-eyed Americans cannot recruit Arabs, or for that matter any other race or ethnic background different from their own; that people naturally are attracted only to others of the same ethnicity. My experience conducting CI around the world confirms the opposite as the norm. In most countries, especially tribal cultures, persons often mistrust those of the same culture and a shared ethnic background can form an obstacle. Natives know too well the web of betrayal common in their own society. Potential recruits are often wary of, in this case, other Arabs, and are more willing to trust the stereotypical American with their safety, as Americans still hold a reputation of honesty and integrity that is at once mysterious and magnetic to other cultures. Of course, a natural advantage of an American Arab trying to deal with an Iraqi Arab is the knowledge of culture, but a non-Arab, savvy to the local culture cancels out such an advantage. In some cases, foreigners insist on talking to an American, refusing to speak in front of someone of the same ethnicity out of concerns for their personal security. Still others derive a sense of status in dealing directly with Americans.

As Ahmed relaxed, he revealed so many interesting allegations it was difficult to determine if there was any truth in them or whether he just fabricated what he thought I wanted to hear. I decided to begin by documenting six potentially verifiable allegations. If those six checked out it would lend credibility to his other statements. One, was a statement that Selah, an Arab-American terp who used to work in the Hard Site, was involved in sexual irregularities as well as a scam to extort money from prisoners. In exchange for sexual favors, Selah would place inmates on the prison hospital list. Once transferred, prisoners could more easily escape or pay additional bribe money to be released. In fact, I learned later that 38 prisoners had escaped that day from a bus transporting them from Abu Ghraib to Rusaffa prison in Baghdad. Allegedly, there were not enough handcuffs for all the prisoners and the Iraqi guards may have been involved in the escape, at least that's what CNN reported. It wasn't difficult to believe that under the guise of too few handcuffs certain prisoners were transferred unshackled. For a few well-placed Dinars, Iraqi guards might look the other way allowing the unshackled prisoners to escape. Considering the failed administration of the prison the escapees might not even be missed.

This raised another potential problem of how an Iraqi national terp gained the power to transfer prisoners to the hospital list. Such action would require contacts with other dishonest persons within the prison and relates to the general issue of corrupt terps, which I discussed earlier.

Ahmed alleged that Selah had been kicked out of the Hard Site and moved to a position at the front gate. That was something I could easily verify. In addition, Ahmed alleged Selah was continuing his scam at the front gate, offering deals to crooked ICOs as they entered the facility. He would instruct cooperative ICOs to seek out prisoners willing to pay for a transfer. Ahmed added that Selah had a friend Abdul who also worked the scam and had been transferred to the gate with Selah. That was something else which could be simply checked.

Later in the day, I learned from the S-2 that Selah was already fired for using his position in the Hard Site to coerce ICOs into sexual relations. Even worse, while working at the front gate, he had intentionally mistranslated incriminating documents found on ICOs entering the prison. This matter should have been fully investigated and Selah thoroughly interrogated. Instead of following through with the possible CI implications, Selah was simply fired and allowed to leave without questioning. Checking with a few colleagues in the Green Zone, I learned that Selah had recently turned up at Titan HQ's in Baghdad to collect his final paycheck. Quickly contacting the Titan manager in charge of Selah, I asked him to hold Selah's paycheck until we could roll him up and question him. Even delaying a few hours could have been sufficient. The manager might have simply asked Selah to return the following day, by then we would have been waiting for him. Incredibly, the manager refused to cooperate because it would not be fair to the employee. Thinking of any means to stop Selah from getting away I tried to contact the nearest U.S. Army Tactical HUMINT Team (THT) in that area but could not reach anyone.

Selah slipped away and dropped from the radar screen, at least for a while. It was frustrating to see an individual like this get away and it was the first of many times I would discover contractors sacrificing the security of our troops to protect their employees and profits. Selah escaped, probably to work another day at a different location, possibly with a new identity. Strangely enough, Abdul too disappeared, failing to show up for work.

It was not a stretch of the imagination to understand that Selah could have easily arranged for insurgent prisoners to transfer and escape for money. We will never know the full extent of Selah's damage or if he had worked with insurgents within the civilian community but at least I knew Ahmed's information so far had been correct, albeit dated.

Ahmed went on to provide other gems of intelligence value. Based on kernels of information he described, we were able to piece together several small but effective operations to try to stem the tide of corruption within the prison. Drug smuggling into Abu Ghraib remained a serious problem. We knew the ICOs were deeply involved and we generated an operation against a specific ICO because one of the prisoners he regularly delivered drugs to was originally arrested for making IEDs. If we could catch him it could prevent another incident or possibly lead us to other insurgents. But before we could catch that ICO, another one became tangled in our web.

64

During a routine search at the front gate, alert Marine guards had caught an ICO trying to smuggle drugs into the prison to sell to inmates. This particular ICO used an ingenious method of mixing narcotics in pill form with candy, but an extra curious Marine spotted two suspicious pieces and reported it. Kudos to the Marine for sure. Unfortunately, the CI agent who initially responded had bungled the entire case so badly I didn't know if we could salvage it. Our agent didn't even bother to check the actual evidence.

He interviewed the ICO called Ibrahim, a thin, quiet man who teared easily. Ibrahim convinced the agent that he was innocent, promising to provide information in the future if the agent would release him now. He swore knowing nothing about the drugs and claimed he was a victim of circumstances. Never considering that as soon as he was released, Ibrahim would certainly disappear never to return again, the young agent worked toward a speedy release. Luckily, the S-2 office would have none of it and asked me to intervene. My first task involved a trip to the evidence locker. Sgt. Wilhelm operated a makeshift room constructed of plywood and chain link fence with rows of wooden shelves inside. It wasn't the fanciest or most secure storage I had seen but considering we were in a war zone in Saddam Hussein's old prison I guess it was good enough. Sgt. Wilhelm brought out three containers of what appeared as standard candy boxed and individually wrapped in cellophane. After examining the evidence closely we discovered large doses of drugs cleverly wrapped along with legitimate sweets.

I quickly halted the release of Ibrahim and following further interview the ICO admitted the extent of his drug operation. Realizing he had been duped the first time, the young agent took it personally and compounded the problem by going back in to talk to Ibrahim, whining that this drug dealer had betrayed his trust. It was immature and unprofessional but the young agent was under the delusion that an Iraqi drug dealer, he had met only hours before, had intimately bonded with him and would confide the absolute truth. Ultimately, the "candy man" as we later called him, went from guard to inmate in a very short time.

6   TORTURE AND COERCION

With the rise of Islamic based terrorism, the face of war as we know it changed dramatically. America faces an enemy that abides no rules and follows no guidelines except the religious doctrine that has been twisted to their own purposes. Under the old rules, combatants spared women and children from the conflict. Islamic terrorists not only use women and children as shields, but also recruit them to become human bombs to kill other women and children in the hopes of breaking the will of civilized societies. In previous conflicts, combatants honored hospitals and Red Cross vehicles as non-targets. Modern terrorists use hospitals as shields for themselves and target the clinics of their enemies. Eventually, they even resorted to using the mentally retarded as suicide bombers. Civilized countries were careful not to destroy historical sites and religious structures during combat. Our current enemy hides within mosques hoping we will attack so they can blame our side for violating rules of war that only apply to us. Meanwhile, they raid and destroy the churches of their enemy without remorse or apology.

The war on Islamic terrorism has changed the entire notion of the battlefield. Gone are the days of the front line and rear area.

Iraq and Afghanistan demonstrated there is no rear area. Every place in the war zone is at war. No one is safe from random attacks that can strike anywhere or hit anyone. Finally, and possibly most interestingly, combating our new enemy has raised the question of how we gather information. It has forced a free society to review the methods it uses to interrogate prisoners of all types. Some skeptics within American society have questioned the methods and philosophy of U.S. military and intelligence agencies.

Is there a difference between soldiers and terrorists? Do those captured in this war on terror enjoy rights similar to Americans? What limits to force should be placed on obtaining information from captives? These questions have mostly been framed for Americans via biased media exaggerations and misrepresentations. In this section, I will try to place these questions and more, before Americans realistically and logically for them to form intelligent opinions on their own.

In the following pages I will try to describe scenarios based on actual situations but modified to present different possible interrogation methods. Names and other facts have been altered to protect methods and information that might be valuable to the enemy. Ultimately, I will ask readers to consider several situations and decide if the methods are reasonable and should be permitted or unreasonable and prohibited. Should certain methods be permitted generally or restricted to approval by high levels of the military or civilian establishment? In this way, I don't think there has ever been a book written like it. I hope by presenting this material we can raise the level of discussion on the subject of coercive interrogation versus the nasty subject of torture.

Let's begin with a brief discussion of the terms *coercion* and *torture*. Mention torture several years ago and it would have conjured images of medieval devices like the rack, where sadistic men in a dark dungeon tied their captive to a table that allowed his feet and hands to be pulled in opposite directions by a crank until the excruciating pain forced him to confess to his captors. The Vietnam War era exposed Americans to oriental brutalities such as placing captives' heads in cages with hungry rats or binding captives' arms behind their backs and suspending them from the ceiling while subjecting them to terrible beatings. Exposure to Saddam Hussein's methods of interrogation demonstrated the extent to which evil man's mind can reach in its imaginations. Saddam and his henchmen drew amusement from dark methods such as boiling in oil, lowering captives into shredding machines, or throwing them from atop tall buildings. In fact, they videotaped various torture sessions for posterity. He also resorted to lesser forms of torture such as electrocution of the genitals, clipping tongues, lopping off ears, gouging out eyes, or chopping off fingers. Islamic terrorists have even added to such misery with the ultimate punishment—beheading.

I want to take a moment to talk of beheading because it is a particularly brutal form of killing. Most Americans probably think of beheading through historical imagery like the guillotine of France or an axe man chopping off the head of a convicted criminal with one sharp blow. With our terrorist enemies, this is far from reality. If you have not seen their method of beheading, I encourage you to look for video of it on the internet. If you can make it through the entire scene you will be changed for life. Modern Islamic terrorists do not chop off the head for a quick, less painful death. They saw off the victim's head with a knife. The process takes what seems to be an eternity all the while the victim is choking and gagging feeling the most severe pain as he dies. As the terrorist struggles to saw through the neck bone the victim seems to suffer the most until his head is completely severed and falls to the floor.

It is difficult enough to watch but imagine for a moment the type of person who would carry out such a task. Imagine the mindset of this person. Now imagine trying to interrogate this person. Do you think it would be different extracting information from this hardened terrorist than it would from other men? Not every captive is a hardened terrorist but consider that such men do exist in numbers. These terrorists require different techniques than ordinary men, to extract intelligence in a timely manner. In fact, interrogation techniques must vary from person to person based on individual weaknesses and vulnerabilities. Personal thresholds for cooperation vary widely as does the skill of interrogators.

As we have seen, interrogation methods are only limited by man's imagination, yet that creative power can work for good or for evil. What qualifies as good or evil? What lines do we draw as a society? Recently, American politicians grappled over these lines. Unfortunately, their arguments were clumsy and influenced more by emotion than logic. Participants in the discussion were not familiar with actual interrogations but versions represented to them by those with specific agendas which too often did not include the safety of our troops and the ability to gather knowledge that would allow us to defeat our enemies. Arguments were also influenced by abuses, though exaggerated and mischaracterized, that left a powerful imprint on the minds of citizens as well as their representatives.

Images from Abu Ghraib prison, splashed across newspaper front pages and TV news screens for months on end, did more to damage honest discussion than the acts themselves. Americans were persuaded that abuse was the normal practice. Distinctions were rarely drawn that the abusers were authorized merely to guard not interrogate prisoners. One person cited was a contract translator, neither authorized to interrogate anyone or order others to do so.[7] The press refused to mention that in our system those who abused prisoners were punished as opposed to our enemies who

---

[7] Jaffe, Gregg, David S. Cloud, and Jonathan Karp. "Titan Worker is Cited in Iraq Scandal." Wall Street Journal. 21 May 2004. 3 August 2008 <http://online.wsj.com/article/SB108509378596117470.html?mod=home_whats_news_us>.

encourage abuse. These and other dangerous moral equivalences confused the public and spoiled honest debate.

In the scenarios below, I will try to differentiate between torture and coercive techniques. There are those so confused on this issue that they deem all coercion as torture. Yet I will argue there are clear differences at either end of the continuum and ways to draw straight lines where previously they were blurred. As I have written in newspaper pieces, Americans clearly see the difference between making a prisoner kneel for 15 minutes and forcing him to kneel for 48 hours. Those who think that all coercion is torture would prohibit all kneeling, a subcategory of what has become known as stress positions. Those who mistakenly draw a moral equivalence between the two would hamstring interrogators who could gather information vital to the war effort.

First, let's discuss the UN and U.S. definition of torture spelled out in the UN Convention Against Torture and other Cruel, Inhuman or Degrading Treatment or Punishment, Article 1, the Military Commission Act of 2006 and Title 18 of the U.S. Code.

UN Convention:

For the purposes of this convention, torture means any act by severe pain or suffering, whether physical or mental, is intentionally inflicted on a person for such purposes as obtaining from him or a third person information or a confession, punishing him for an act he or a third person has

72

committed or is suspected of having committed, or intimidating or coercing him or a third person or for any reason based on discrimination of any kind, when such pain or suffering is inflicted by or at the instigation of or with the consent or acquiescence of a public official or other person acting in an official capacity. It does not include pain or suffering arising only from, inherent in or incidental to lawful sanctions.

Military Commission Act of 2006

§ 950v. Crimes triable by military commissions

(b) OFFENSES;

(11) TORTURE –

(A) OFFENSE–Any person… who commits an act specifically intended to inflict severe physical or mental pain or suffering (other than pain or suffering incidental to lawful sanctions), upon another person within his custody or physical control for the purpose of obtaining information or a confession, punishment, intimidation or coercion, or any reason based on discrimination of any kind, shall be punished, if death results to one or more of the victims, by death or such other punishment as a military commission under this chapter may direct…

"Severe mental pain or suffering" is defined in 18 U.S.C. Section 2340 (2):

Title 18 U.S.C. Section 2340 (1), (2)

(1) "torture" means an act committed by a person acting under the color of law specifically intended to inflict severe physical or mental pain or suffering (other than pain or suffering incidental to lawful sanctions) upon another person within his custody or control

(2) "severe mental pain and suffering" means the prolonged mental harm caused by or resulting from –

(A) the intentional infliction or threatened infliction of severe physical pain or suffering;

(B) the administration or application, or threatened administration or application, of mind altering substances or other procedures calculated to disrupt profoundly the senses or the personality;

(C) the threat of imminent death; or

(D) the threat that another person will imminently be subjected to death, severe physical pain or suffering, or the administration or application, of mind altering substances or other procedures calculated to disrupt profoundly the senses or the personality...

Before we begin the discussion of interpreting this convention by elements who have agreed to abide by it we must not forget the argument that our enemy is not a party to this Convention and, one could argue, should not enjoy the benefits of its protection.

As stated previously, our enemy is not an Army, wears no uniform, follows no rules recognized by us and in fact, violates both the letter and the spirit of every aspect of the Convention. So, it is logical to argue that in the case of terrorists the Convention should not apply. Of course, the counter argument most commonly used is that the U.S. must take the high ground, forever observing the spirit of the Convention even when our adversary does not. Others would argue that it is easy to stand on principle while engaged in theoretical academic discourse spouted from the safety of American soil but not so simple when faced with actual life and death situations in a war zone. It is easy to demand we fight with one arm tied behind our back if you are not the combatant.

A third group insists it is reasonable to argue that the U.S. can claim the moral high ground while still allowing exceptions when in the best interest of the lives of Americans in harms way. Such exceptions may require high-level approval but should exist nonetheless. In other words, there may be times when clear torture is justified and we should acknowledge so. I actually argue that Americans should never acknowledge or accept torture because it unjustly paints us in the same category as our enemy or other barbarous regimes. We must however, distinguish between coercive methods and torture. We cannot allow coercive methods such as stress positions, sleep deprivation, hooding and dozens of others to be classified as torture. Such a philosophical surrender would allow enemies of America to draw moral equivalences between safe and effective interrogation methods and actual torture which would cause coercive measures to be outlawed along with torture. These arguments will become apparent as we proceed.

Still others, such as Senator John McCain, argue against torture from another angle. Former POWs such as McCain offer a compelling argument to those who respect the service of our military men and women. McCain and his ilk insist that if we subject terrorists to "torture," that our troops would be subjected to the same treatment. McCain's stature is enough to convince those who have little knowledge of the crux of the argument. "If John McCain said so then that's good enough for me," I have heard a number of well-intentioned citizens say. There are four strong fallacies to the McCain argument, the first of which is that we all agree—everyone is against torture. As I stated earlier, I think it is counterproductive to argue FOR torture. Americans in large numbers are against inhumane treatment of prisoners, but what is inhumane? Those who would classify all coercion as torture are hurting America's effort.

The second fallacy is that these terrorists are military prisoners subject to Geneva Convention protection. As stated earlier, terrorists are not military personnel, do not wear uniforms, do not follow military rules of war, and thus do not, and should not, qualify for protection under the Convention.

The third fallacy is that not affording terrorists Geneva Convention protection affects the treatment of American soldiers captured by the enemy in future wars. Not affording terrorists Convention protection in no way affects the treatment of Americans fighting other militaries in some future war. American soldiers fighting against another country's military would still be able to expect treatment according to the rules of the Convention assuming we are fighting an actual military force, and that country recognizes the Convention.

The final fallacy is that somehow our treatment by terrorists or even rogue nation military units would change because of our current treatment of terrorists. Here's the news flash: OUR TROOPS DO NOT RECEIVE SUCH TREATMENT NOW. Terrorists BEHEAD prisoners. It is ludicrous to believe that our treatment of terrorists truly influences their behavior. Even during Vietnam where McCain served, we WERE fighting a military force and we did treat prisoners well but by McCain's own admission THEY did not. The so-called McCain argument is wrapped in emotion not logic.

Let's return to the definition of torture itself. As we can see there are several ambiguous words within that definition that allow broad interpretation. Most assuredly, it was written as such to convince a variety of countries to agree on the wording knowing that they could continue their operations without interruption based on that country's particular interpretation. The two words I will focus on that cause the most trouble are *severe* and *threats*. Severe pain can be interpreted from multiple perspectives. The threshold of pain varies among individuals. Who can then say what is severe? Each country can determine what it judges as severe, creating a number of standards among nations with no clear international agreement, which is what we are faced with today. *Severe* has and should be defined by our country as long lasting pain that leaves permanent physical damage. Such a definition forbids maiming, amputations, scarring, and mutilation, which the U.S. already prohibits. A definition so stated is reasonable and permits coercive techniques below that level. As policy, we did permit coercive techniques by trained personnel under supervision and approval of designated authority. Those were adequate safeguards that permitted our troops the latitude needed to accomplish the mission in a way acceptable to the values of American society.

Another argument raised by opponents is that we should ban all forms of coercion and torture because they do not work. The example most commonly cited is that a prisoner will confess to anything in order for the procedure to stop. This is such a flimsy argument that whenever I hear it I immediately suspect it comes from someone unfamiliar with interrogation or unschooled in its use. Both coercion and torture can fail if improperly administered. In fact, even the simplest technique can fail if the interrogator is not skilled. Simply stated, there are effective interrogators and ineffective ones, yet somehow their arguments are allowed to carry the same weight. In any profession, if the worker claimed he could do all jobs with the same tool and the other tools did not work, one would immediately suspect he either did not know how to use the other tools or that he was not an expert in his trade. The same principle applies in interrogation. Tools can become quite specialized. No one tool is used in every circumstance and all tools have their place. Let's return to the argument about confessing to anything. Of course, given enough pain you could make me confess to killing Abraham Lincoln, but it would not be the truth. Skilled interrogators seek the truth. Successful coercive techniques are delivered after mentally preparing the prisoner, informing him that the technique will continue until the information he provides can be verified, so the sooner he delivers truthful information the better for him. I prefer the example of the suspect picked up after he was caught planting an IED along the road. From evidence captured with him we learned he planted several others before his capture. It is imperative those IEDs be found quickly before lives are lost. As the techniques are applied the information is confirmed. If the suspect admits to planting a second IED on the corner of Monsour Street and Third Avenue then a patrol is radioed to check it out. If he is truthful then the technique is halted, if not it continues. The basic premise is that if the technique is effective the suspect will begin by confessing the truth. There is no reason to prolong his situation by continuing to lie. A suspect may lie initially to test the interrogator's will or ability, but the test of wills quickly collapses if the interrogator keeps up the pressure.

What about water boarding? Language is important here. The term really describes a procedure with varying applications and different degrees to which it can be applied. We must define what we mean by water boarding. The basic principal involves strapping an individual to a board and pouring water over the air entry points to simulate drowning. It produces a type of gag reflex that while quite frightening is not dangerous if done properly. Like any other skill, to appropriately administer it requires training and medical supervision. It is not intended for use on the average suspect who wets himself when yelled at. It is applied to hardened killers who have been trained to resist coercive interrogation methods and take joy in sawing off their victims' heads. Performed professionally, there is no substantial risk of death or permanent injury. Should a provision to use this technique on terrorists be authorized in specific circumstances?

Almost every technique can be abused. Let's consider tazing for a moment. Few people object to its use in controlling unruly suspects, but I don't think Americans would agree to its use in interrogation. The point is, there are techniques below the threshold of torture that are effective when used appropriately and not abused.

From the media coverage, one might expect that water boarding is a routine interrogation tactic. Based on media and Hollywood mischaracterizations, Americans are led to believe thousands of innocent Iraqis are subjected to water boarding or

80

other extreme measures during detention. In fact, recent testimony before Congress confirmed this much-maligned technique has only been used three times since 9/11.[8] Once on Khalid Sheik Mohamed, the mastermind of the 9/11, who held out the longest—a whopping two minutes. Reportedly, after the short session he began to talk so much interrogators could hardly keep up with him. He explained in detail how he killed reporter Daniel Pearl, by slitting his throat. He revealed inside information on Al Qaeda including details that allowed us to capture or neutralize other terrorists. After one session of water boarding, Khalid never needed coercion again, but willingly cooperated with his captors.

Another water boarding alum, Abu Zubaydah was captured in Pakistan and after only 34 seconds reportedly provided valuable information in the war on terror. Interestingly enough Zubaydah previously instructed others on how to resist interrogation methods. This hardened terrorist, a man who had suffered the pain of gunshot wounds to the stomach and groin could not withstand one half a minute under the spigot.

---

[8] Mikkelsen, Randall. "CIA says used waterboarding on three suspects." Reuters. 5 Feb 2008. 23 July 2008 <http://www.reuters.com/article/topNews/idUSN0517815120080205?feedType=RSS&feedName=topNews>.

The third recipient was Al Nashiri, accused of assisting in the bombing of the U.S.S. Cole Destroyer on 12 October 2000 in the Yemen port known as Aden, killing 17 sailors. It is not known how long he lasted under the technique. While considered one of the most coercive techniques, its use is limited to the most resistant terrorists withholding perishable intelligence. It is one tool in the interrogation tool kit so to speak and should not be eliminated.

Human rights groups branded water boarding as "torture" but that should come as no surprise. These same groups consider hooding and kneeling for ten minutes as torture. They would remove every coercive technique from the hands of our interrogators if given the chance. We should not base our policy decisions on the ramblings of those without the knowledge or experience to meaningfully contribute to the debate.

Policy guidelines for interrogation should be based on a clear definition of torture that permits techniques short of those that leave long lasting or permanent physical harm. Allowing opponents to draw moral equivalence between effective tactics such as water boarding and true Saddam-like torture, such as lowering humans into shredding machines or boiling oil, endangers the lives of all Americans and does a disservice to those on the front lines trying to protect us. Our politicians should support coerced interrogations and stop demagoguing the issue.

Who is truly interrogated? In reality, few people are actually interrogated and not everyone is interrogated to the same degree. Like so many terms, the word "interrogation" is one that can be defined in several ways. The military uses it to describe the most harsh interview techniques. Other questioning that Americans might think is interrogation does not qualify. The kind of questioning seen on television police shows is not usually considered interrogation at all. Law enforcement prefers to refer to such questioning as "interviewing."[9] At least two kinds of interviewing are distinct; witness interviewing and subject interviewing. Witness interviewing consists of probing questions designed to elicit information from persons who may have seen a crime or know something of value to an investigation. Witnesses are usually, but not always, cooperative. Subject interviewing can become, but is not necessarily, more confrontational. It involves interviewing the suspect of a crime. These two types of questioning, though specifically not included in the definition of military interrogation are often mistakenly associated with the definition. Even military personnel confuse these distinctions, thinking all questioning is interrogation. In Army terms, the overwhelming percentage of sources, witnesses and suspects are questioned with what is known as the direct approach. This

---

[9] For purposes of discussion in this book, I have used the two terms interview and interrogation interchangeably.

involves direct questioning of an individual without using any ruses or ploys to gain cooperation. Only a small percentage are questioned using other types of methods like the incentive approach, the emotional approach, good guy/bad guy, file and dossier, or any of the other seventeen basic approaches taught to Army interrogators.

For our purposes it is important because knowledge of the distinctions helps answer the question of who is interrogated. One of the objections most often posed by those lacking knowledge about how interrogation is conducted in a war zone deals with the capture of innocents. "Why are so many innocent people interrogated?" is one form of the questions commonly asked. "Look at the number of innocent people the military finally sets free, that is a shame those people were wrongly accused," is another form of the misunderstanding common among citizens. Let's examine an example based on a real life situation that might help clear up this point of contention.

A military patrol roaming the city begins to receive small arms fire from a few nearby buildings. It appears shots are coming from several windows or maybe from persons moving between windows in the buildings. After taking casualties, the patrol calls for backup, effectively surrounds two buildings and captures everyone inside. About 25 people in all, including women and children are taken captive. On the scene, soldiers, possibly including one trained in military intelligence, begin the first filter,

84

questioning to sort out who might be actually involved, who might know about those involved and who knows nothing of value. For the purpose of this example, let's say there were actually three insurgents firing from the buildings, but we do not know that yet. We must consider that among those taken captive, gender and age mean little. Women and even children could have been the shooters or have been directly helping them. Others may have been related to the shooter, providing the use of their apartment or place of business from which to conduct the ambush. Still others may have seen something but are too afraid to say anything to the American soldiers for fear the insurgents will return later and kill them. This is not a situation easily sorted out.

The group of 25 is separated as much as possible and questioning begins. One middle-aged lady is screaming and crying that she was taken captive. "I have done nothing, I have done nothing why have you arrested me?" She has two small children and is naturally worried for their care and safety. She tells one soldier that a man with a brown outer garment and a red headscarf was one of the insurgents but she did not see anyone else. The woman believes he was an insurgent because she saw him enter an apartment on the second floor with an AK-47 rifle and he does not live in the building. She informs the soldiers that a man named Ahmed Ali lives there.

A young boy shyly tells the soldiers that three men came to one building together in a white four-door car parked on the side of the building. He describes them briefly. Another person also saw the three men enter the apartment of Mohammed Abdullah. Other soldiers, actually interviewing Mohammed, recorded he knew nothing about any men entering the building. After about an hour of preliminary questioning, the soldiers decide that 20 people have knowledge or were involved. It will take time to record, cross check the stories and verify the information. We must also consider that soldiers are not police, neither are they trained in questioning or law enforcement interviews. The scene is chaotic as is normal and the area too dangerous to continue there so all 20 of the original 25 are taken back to the base for more questioning. So far five have been released. All we know at this point is the remaining persons include witnesses, innocents and probably at least one suspect. As the group arrives at the base they are taken to a processing center where a team of interpreters and a few screeners can record their personal data. In this case, the local counterintelligence unit is called and two agents respond to help sort out the situation. A few of the soldiers originally fired upon still have hot tempers as they strongly suspect the people shooting at them and ultimately killing one of their comrades are among this group. They want them identified and punished without delay.

Almost immediately the second layer of filtering begins. CI agents review the information collected thus far, interviewing the soldiers to add their stories to the mix and clarify points raised in their initial reports. They try to keep the people separated as much

86

as possible but there are not appropriate facilities available. Military Police help separate a few of the men they believe to be suspects into holding cells. The entire group must be guarded at all times. Even those who are considered witnesses might be insurgents posing as witnesses to throw off the investigation with false information. The clock is ticking and everything must be completed quickly and we must decide who to release or detain for further questioning. In reality, the soldiers would like to complete as much interviewing as possible that day because detaining people overnight presents additional difficulty. All detainees must be fed and guarded consuming valuable personnel and tomorrow will bring another day with more patrols and possibly new prisoners. Unfortunately, this group was brought in late in the afternoon so the agents have even less time to work with. They begin by interviewing the women with children to eliminate suspects and allow the innocent to leave quickly. Detention of women and children causes the most tension in the Muslim community and are the most difficult to care for as far as food and amenities. If this were America, we could just record their names and ask them to return the following day for further questioning, but this is Iraq. Once those citizens are released, they will never be heard from again so everything must be completed prior to release.

Three more residents identified the man with the brown outer garment and they were released, as were a half-dozen others who convinced the CI agents they had no further information to provide. The man with the brown outer garment previously identified as carrying an AK-47 into the apartment of Ahmed Ali, is brought in for questioning. He admits his friendship with Ahmed Ali and claims he was bringing him a weapon for personal protection. The man is cooperative and says when the shooting started both he and Ahmed hid hoping the insurgents would not break into Ahmed's apartment but they were prepared to defend themselves. He insists the AK-47 was never fired and described where it was left in the apartment. His story is believable and can be verified but it will take time. We will have to send a patrol back into the dangerous area to retrieve the weapon and also search the car described by other witnesses. This takes time and in the meantime the man will have to be held until his story can be verified. He is not at all happy but after further explanation, he seems to understand the necessity from our point of view.

Ahmed Ali relates the same story as the man in the brown outer garment. Because Ahmed lives in a dangerous neighborhood he purchased an AK-47 to protect his home and family. This is normal for most Iraqis.

A few of the residents identified the three men who did not live in the apartments. They also identified Mustafa as a friend of Mohammed who lives in the second building. Four more persons are released that evening leaving seven persons to be detained overnight until more information can be gathered; Mohammed, Mustafa, the three men, Ahmed and the man with the brown outer garment. Everyone calls it quits for the night hoping to start fresh in the morning. A dawn patrol is organized to return to the buildings to gather evidence.

Early the next morning, Mustafa is interviewed and swears he knows nothing of the three men and barely knows Mohammed even though his neighbors reported they were close friends. The three men said they knew no one in the buildings but were simply passing through when the shooting started and took refuge in the building. They complained bitterly of their innocence.

That afternoon the special patrol returns with the AK-47 from Ahmed's apartment and evidence taken from the white car identified as belonging to the three men believed to be the shooters. The AK-47 is still in its wrappings and has never been fired. Ahmed and his friend are released shortly after. Thoroughly searching the entire building, the patrol also discovered a cache of weapons in the basement, which residents said belonged to Mustafa. The remaining five men are considered to be concealing information and are scheduled for interrogation. The rest of the day is spent preparing to talk to the men, running their names through databases and comparing information from all the interviews gathered.

The third day is important because we must determine if we will continue to detain or release the remaining persons. Further detention requires justification before sending them on to the Division Interrogation Facility (DIF). At the DIF, suspects can remain 30 days before a new determination to send them on to Abu

Ghraib or a similar prison for up to six months. New interrogators
at the DIF will have more time to probe the suspects either for
additional strategic information or take the time needed to break
them. But we are still dealing with them at the tactical level, trying
to discover who was involved in the ambush two days before.

One by one the three men were interviewed. They carried
no identification but identified themselves as Salim, Hussein and
Yousif. Salim was Kurdish not Arab and so we wondered why he
traveled with the other two. In the first round of interrogation all
three stuck to their stories. Hussein was a tough young man with
several scars he said he received in childhood accidents. Yousif was
also hardened, continually on the offensive, accusing the
interrogators of human rights abuse while demanding his immediate
release. On the second round of questioning in the afternoon, Salim
complained his family would be worrying about him. His eyes
grow teary as he speaks. Interrogators pounce telling Salim that he
is in deep trouble and if he does not tell the entire truth he will be
turned over to the Kurdish Peshmerga forces and will likely be
killed for assisting the insurgency. Salim breaks down into a full
cry. He does not want to die, and begins to reveal a bit of his role,
confessing the other two men are not who they say but are actually
from Syria. The one called Hussein is actually named Khalim.
Salim does not know Yousif's true name. Salim admits he helped
Hussein and Yousif to hide in Kurdish territory, away from U.S.
patrols. The two men paid him well and the money helped Salim's

family buy food and medicine. He tells the interrogators that the two men have connections to other insurgents in the Al Zarqawi ring. Salim did not learn all the details but knew the others were planning a major ambush of U.S. Forces in the next two weeks, involving several cells of insurgents equipped with IEDs, RPGs and other lethal weapons. Salim confessed that at least one cache of weapons remained hidden just across the border in Kurdish territory. The location of the other caches was unknown to him. Interrogators worked with maps to pinpoint a description of the weapons cache location. Information Salim provided could be verified but it would take time. Salim provided one more important piece of info, a third person, the actual leader of the group, had escaped. His name was Fawaz, no last names were ever used among the group.

Let's pause here to examine a potential problem with the procedures used in this scenario. The interrogators may have committed two egregious violations according to our previous definition of torture. They threatened the suspect with death and threatened to turn him over to forces that might torture or kill him. If you interpret the rules strictly, threats of death are prohibited. This brings us to the question of how to define and interpret "threats of death." Let's begin at the far end of the continuum to try and reach agreement. If an interrogator intended to cause death, let's say by placing a loaded gun to Salim's head and cocking it, might that be a form of torture? What if we hung Salim over a pit of venomous snakes and slowly lowered him into it? Might that qualify as a threat of death that constituted torture? But let's also consider for a moment, situations where in fact no threat exists but we want to convince the suspect that the threat is real. Return to the scenario with the loaded gun. What if the gun was not loaded but Salim did not know it? Should that be prohibited? Let's move further down the continuum. What if, as in the scenario above, the interrogators had no intention of turning over Salim to the Peshmerga, and of course had no way of knowing if the Pesh would kill him, should that threat also be prohibited? Should it be prohibited to trick or frighten a suspect? If so, are there any acceptable methods of trickery? Should there be? This is a question Americans must consider. I believe average Americans would have no problem with the methods used to break Salim into providing vital information that might save American lives in battle. Interrogators should have the means available to elicit information from insurgents, suspects or terrorists. What limits, if any, should be placed on interrogators? The issue in its true complexity has not been explained to the American people or debated fairly in public. Coercion is a subject easily sensationalized and the media takes full advantage of the opportunity. Congressmen often demagogue the issue out of ignorance or too often, for political gain.

Salim had provided valuable tactical info but for certain he remained of high intelligence value. Having assisted actual insurgents for several months he could provide critical information on methods, personnel, hiding places, and a stream of other topics of use to Coalition Forces. Once again, this process would take time.

Salim possessed intelligence value beyond the tactical needs of the unit concerned with the upcoming ambush. He will be sent to a higher echelon interrogation facility where trained interrogators can work on him for extended periods, drawing out valuable intelligence information that may help identify other insurgents or supporters, methods of operation, and additional information as described above. Since Salim has been cooperative there is likely no longer a need to use coercive techniques in further interrogation. Rapport building methods may be instituted to help gain Salim's continued cooperation over the long term.

Rapport building is a useful interrogation method perfected in law enforcement to gain the cooperation of suspects. Using rapport building, the interrogator finds commonalities that can help bond him with the suspect, earning the suspect's trust. This method often takes longer periods of time to become effective and does not work in all cases. It is best used in strategic situations where long-term confinement may work to the advantage of the interrogators. Unfortunately, some interrogators who work in strategic intelligence interrogations and use this method almost exclusively mistakenly think it is the only method of value. Their focused experience has blinded them to other methods used effectively in different situations. Most military interrogators work in situations such as the prison environment where time is a minimal factor. In those situations, coercive methods lose value and may even prove counterproductive. Rapport building emerges as a more useful tool. However, coercive techniques should not be disregarded even in these situations. The choice of method always centers on the person, the skill of the interrogator and the situation.

But let's return to our hypothetical example. Time is still a factor and this time Hussein was brought in for another round of interrogation. One guard from the patrol mentioned that during the capture of Hussein he reacted strangely to the military guard dogs at the checkpoint. The Sergeant said that Hussein tried to hide his fear but recoiled at the site of the dogs and attempted to hide behind Yousif, an astute observation that would prove valuable to an interrogator.

Hussein entered the interrogation room bold and arrogant. Immediately he began demanding his release and his rights, also complaining that his handcuffs were too tight and that we were abusing him. If nothing else, such behavior raised suspicion that Hussein had been coached on what to do if captured by Americans. Shepherds are usually unworldly and know little about American rights or interrogation methods. Hussein seemed comfortable in his current situation indicating that he had either been there before or had received training on the interrogation process and how to resist it. The initial questioning went badly. Hussein refused to answer any questions insisting that he was innocent and American occupiers were abusing him. He denied knowledge of any shootings. After several hours of questioning, Hussein was showing little signs of wear. We decided to test the affect of the dog on him. We began by just a simple display of the dog, a muscular German police dog named Viper, used for sentry duty. Sgt Michaels, the handler, brought him in the room and had him sit about eight feet away facing Hussein while we observed his reaction. As soon as Hussein caught sight of the dog he began fidgeting and moving back in his chair. He began to object but after only a few words Viper barked at him. The echo in the room amplified the bark causing Hussein to freeze. I explained that the dog was quite disciplined but would tolerate no shenanigans (don't know how the interpreter translated that) telling him that Viper was a good judge of character and could actually detect human lies. Sgt Michaels stood behind Hussein charged with signaling the dog to bark or growl if I pursed my lips, which would mean Hussein had told a lie. I told Hussein we would conduct a little test to demonstrate our dog's ability. I would begin by asking known questions, staring with Hussein's age, to which he responded 25, no reaction from the dog. I asked him if he knew Ali and he said yes, again no reaction from the dog. I then told him to purposely lie to demonstrate Viper's ability. I asked him what day it was and Hussein said it was Monday, which was in error. Sgt Michaels knew enough to signal Viper to bark and jerk toward Hussein about a step. Viper remained several feet away but the approach not only surprised Hussein, it convinced him the dog actually detected his lie. Hussein remained visibly uncomfortable that the dog was even in the room. Frequently shifting in his seat he would wince from time to time. Now, we began the ultimate effect.

"As you can see our canine friend cannot only detect your lies but he thoroughly dislikes liars. If you continue to deceive us we will have increasing difficulty restraining him. I will continue with easy questions and move toward the more difficult. What is your name?" I asked matter-of-factly.

Hussein paused and answered "Hussein."

Almost imperceptibly I pursed my lips and Sgt. Michaels signaled Viper to bark loudly and become agitated.

"That's odd," I said while getting up off the table. "It appears you are lying again. You have not been honest about your name. What is your name?"

Sgt Michaels made Viper growl a little, even showing his teeth without my cue.

"Quickly, before I let Viper have his way with you."

Hussein was now in a frenzy. He knew he was lying but did not know how Viper could know. The growling dog was unnerving him.

"Khalim" he stuttered, "my name is Khalim."

"Oh really?" I said with a cocked head and raised eyebrows. "Maybe we should leave you alone with Viper for a few minutes to convince you to tell the truth from the beginning."

Hussein turned his body sideways in the chair and said, "No, no, I will tell you what I know."

From that point, Hussein began to reveal how he and his comrades had waited to attack the patrol and then escape. He provided several bits of verifiable intelligence and agreed to show us a cache of weapons still hidden near the river.

Once again let's pause and examine this scenario. Should we prohibit employing a known personal fear against a suspect? Should U.S. policy totally restrict ruses and fear to gather information in a time sensitive combat situation? Even if you agree such tactics should be permitted you may still desire limitations. In this case, the dog remained almost eight feet away. What about six feet? Four? What about allowing the dog close enough to sniff the suspect? What about allowing the dog within just a few inches and ordering him to bark and growl? We all remember the pictures of the growling dog shown hundreds of times by the media attempting to smear U.S. soldiers and paint them as evil. Clearly there are limits, but are there legitimate uses? Certainly, most Americans would draw the line at the dog actually biting the suspect, but working backwards from that point, where should we draw the line in this scenario? Fear combined with trickery can be an effective means of gaining information. Both can be used in multiple combinations without long lasting harm to the terrorist.

Should interrogators be allowed to pursue the phobias of suspects in order to gain information? At one time they were authorized. Let's return to the scenario above but instead of intimidating dogs let's substitute spiders. If a suspect had arachnophobia would it be permissible to incorporate a stuffed animal style spider into the interrogation? How about a rubber spider? Could we place the rubber spider close to him? Could we place it on his arm? Now how about a real spider on the table in front of him? Just a small one? As you can see there are countless scenarios we might contrive. Would any of these constitute torture? My point is that I believe the American people would accept scenarios where we used phobias against terrorists to gather information, and since it does not inflict lasting harm it does not rise to the level of torture.

Returning to the more general misperceptions about prisoners in Iraq, are innocents often picked up in the initial action, of course they are. Hopefully, you can see from the above scenario how and why this might happen. Are those people filtered out as quickly as possible? It is in the interest of the soldiers to eliminate innocents if for no other reason than it is a terrible burden trying to care for them while in custody. The American public is never told of this. Conversely, the public is led to believe that American forces trample the rights of citizens without regard to truth, compassion, or civil rights. The reality is quite the opposite.

7 INTERROGATION

One day, without advance notice, Special Forces (SF) showed up with a busload of Sudanese, Nigerians and Somalis. They spoke some English and Arabic. They were mostly Muslims, a few were Christians. Some had been persecuted in their own country and also in Iraq. Most had come to Iraq more than a decade before as menial laborers never returning to their home countries. They were just trying to survive, but all wanted to go to America. They all believed America was their last hope. No matter what Saddam or the insurgents or Al Jazeera said about America, they all knew it was the last hope for all people.

SF asked us to screen them. Of course, none of these men were in the database but our process had become well known as the most rigorous in Iraq, and working closely with Force Protection and our Base Commander, Mosul had developed a reputation as the most secure base in Iraq and units began to rely on us. If there was any doubt in their mind about foreign nationals within their sphere of command they brought them to us for a re-screening. We took our work very seriously and became quite successful in weeding out crooks, disloyal employees, CI threats and other undesirables that had managed to obtain access to U.S. Forces.

THE UNSEEN WAR IN IRAQ

This group presented an interesting challenge because I had never worked against Sudanese, Nigerians or Somalis. Ignorance of the culture places an interrogator at a disadvantage. These were black Africans living in an Arab society. Although most were Muslim, they never really assimilated into Iraqi society. Very few Iraqi women would have any relationship with them and even Iraqi males did not treat them kindly. They were persecuted and relegated to the dirty jobs of Iraq. One advantage for us was they already expected better treatment from Americans and they were eager to please. Whatever time they had spent with SF they had enjoyed and were warm towards Americans. In their short contact with the U.S., their lives had improved dramatically. They cooperated fully in the interviews, which made the screening go much more smoothly for them. Well most of them. Within any group that large there are always bad apples and our job was to find them and weed them out.

Cultural ignorance affects the translator as well as the interrogator. Inexperienced interrogators often make the fatal mistake of assuming the interpreter knows all, that the interpreter speaks native English including its idioms and that the interpreter knows the cultural pitfalls of every suspect. The reality is often quite the opposite. Most interpreters have limited English ability, weak understanding of English idioms and even an uneducated handle on culture and religious differences within their own multi-cultural country. It would be a mistake to assume an Iraqi

100

interpreter can accurately portray messages from African suspects. Cultural differences can include some dramatic distinctions such as when yes means no and vice versa. However, on the battlefield you do the best you can. Interrogating suspects from varied cultures can be detrimental to the accuracy and validity of what's uncovered.

Of course, there are a few basic interrogation tools that are helpful, but few interrogators use them. Supervising other counter-intelligence agents, I have had the opportunity to sit in on plenty of their interviews to help them improve technique. My experience is that few of them actually follow sound fundamentals. Basic questioning technique provides an appropriate example.

Experts teach the five basic types of questions: general/rapport building, follow-up, control, repeat and prepared. General questions are designed to help establish a rapport with the suspect or set the tone of the interview. They can be friendly or firm but it is generally better to start friendly and move to firm. It is difficult to move towards friendly after you have been firm without actually changing interrogators. These questions can range from talking about weather, sports, hometowns, family, etc., anything that might put the person at ease and gain cooperation. Yet, believe it or not, too many interrogators do not spend enough time on this part of the questioning, some skip it completely. Part of the temptation for skipping rapport-building questions rests in the desire to crank out numbers of interviews completed per day. Interrogators in a war zone stay busy, often with far more potential interviews than time to complete them. By skipping or shortening the rapport building segment an interrogator can reduce a two-hour interview to 75 – 90 minutes. Let's say he is required to interview four people per 12-hour day. That allows eight hours for four interviews, an hour for breaks and lunch, and three hours for paperwork. By cutting a 120-minute interview to 75-90 minutes, an interviewer can now either complete four interviews in less time or can conduct more interviews per day making him appear more productive. Both of these approaches carry inherent dangers. The depth of the interviews and information gathered is likely to suffer. When I first arrived in Mosul, I discovered agents conducting two-hour interviews in 15 minutes. This discovery was appalling and put into question the very credibility of the process. As I mentioned before, we discovered a few other locations had become notorious for these perfunctory interviews. Not only did savvy Titan representatives prefer to schedule their prospective translators for screening at the locations with 15-minute interviews, but no doubt the insurgency caught on that to obtain access to U.S. facilities, it would be safer to introduce agents through those same locations.

Even more appalling, when I first arrived in Mosul one of the agents told me that he gave the owner of the local food court, a Turkish businessman, preferential treatment in employee screenings by just pushing them through with abbreviated interviews in return for free meals at the food court. Astoundingly, I had the most difficult time firing this agent for what I personally consider a treasonous act worthy of criminal punishment. Faced with full scrutiny of his employees, the Turkish businessman had the nerve to complain that he no longer received preferential treatment in the screening of his workers. It may be hard for those not in Iraq to believe such scenarios, but my point is there are numerous ways to cut corners in the fundamentals and this is just one.

Follow-up questions are designed to develop information from answers given during an interview. For example, an interrogator asks how many people were with the suspect when he was captured. The suspect replies "Three." The logical follow-up questions: Who were they? What were their names, ages, descriptions? Where were they from? How long did you know them? What were they wearing? Did they carry weapons? What kind? You can see the follow-up questions can continue almost indefinitely. Unfortunately, inexperienced or lazy interrogators neglect follow-up questions or stop short of pursuing the questions to logical conclusions.

The third type of question may be the most important. Control questions are based on known/confirmed information. Interrogators intersperse these questions among unknown questions to test for honesty. Beginning with control questions or, frontloading too many of them, damages the process. Control questions should never be asked directly or it will tip the suspect as to how to answer. For example, you learned from interviewing neighbors that the suspect spent time in Syria. During the interview, your control question would never directly address this point for example, "Have you ever spent time in Syria?" Interrogators try to mask control questions by disguising them in generalities. "Have you traveled outside Baghdad?" Or, "Have you ever traveled abroad?" If he says yes, the follow-up is, "Where?" He may answer with Jordan and Egypt but not Syria. Another follow-up would logically become, "Any other areas beside Jordan and Egypt?" He responds, "No," again. Later you would repeat and triangulate the question making sure he did not forget or misunderstand. It's important that an interrogator leave no way out for the suspect to argue once confronted with his deception. The interrogator must cover all the possible angles of the question.

Repeat questions help test for honesty and accuracy. These are most necessary when translators lack ability or cultural knowledge. Questions may be asked several times to ensure the answers compare. Discrepancies can be attributed to dishonesty or misunderstanding. Triangulating information gained is critical. Repeating a question in a slightly different way is part of this technique. For example, you ask the suspect what time he left home and he replies, 2 o'clock. You follow-up with, "AM or PM?" He says PM. A few questions later you ask, "So you left your house in the morning," posing the question in error to see if the suspect corrects you. You would expect the suspect to answer, "No, as I told you, I left in the afternoon." If he says anything different then you have a problem. Repeat questions are usually posed three times.

Finally, in intelligence circles, prepared questions are derived from standard information being sought at higher levels. They may also come from an interrogation plan prepared before conducting the interview.

All five types of questions have their place in the interview. Some are especially helpful when dealing cross-culturally or with interpreters of varying ability. In addition, interrogators are taught to avoid yes/no questions and ask questions that require a narrative. Simply "Where were you born?" is better than "Were you born in Baghdad?" Questions lending themselves to longer narrative are preferred. "Tell me about your service in the military." "What do you remember about the men you trained with?" These questions allow the suspect to tell a story that can paint a picture further filled in with follow-up questions as you go.

The problem is that interrogators become lazy in the fundamentals and skip important steps often damaging the depth of information received. Of course basic questioning is just one small but important tool in the interrogator's toolbox.

Beyond basic interrogation methods there were a few rules of thumb to remember in Iraq. First, people in this culture stick to the lie. Logic and reason will not dissuade them. Under Saddam any sign of confession could be harmful. Most people know the story of Saddam's two second cousins and sons-in-law who defected in 1995. The two defectors, Saddam Kamel and Hussein Kamel were brothers both married to Saddam's daughters. They held high ranking positions in the Iraqi government. Hussein Kamel cooperated with the CIA and other intelligence organizations secretly. Saddam begged the two to return to Iraq convincing them all would be forgiven and promising a full pardon. Foolishly enough they believed him and returned in 1996 only to be executed.

Interrogators sometimes try to convince suspects that all is forgiven if they tell the truth but wary Iraqis are difficult to convince because Saddam effectively poisoned that pool. The result is they doggedly stick to the lie refusing to admit guilt. This becomes critical because when a person is a convincing liar and insists on his innocence passionately, inexperienced interrogators begin to doubt their own instincts or even the evidence itself. I have seen competent liars convince interrogators of their innocence. It is embarrassing to have to go back in to re-interview and break them but it provides a valuable lesson to inexperienced interrogators. It takes patience and experience but you cannot allow yourself to be fooled by emotional pleas. Interrogators must follow the evidence.

One enormous help in defeating the standoff of competing stories is to develop corroborating information. In the presence of hard evidence, the most emphatic denials lose their effect on the interrogator because his confidence is bolstered by hard evidence.

I remember showing video of a suspect who vehemently denied any involvement. Faced with the video evidence, he continued to deny that the person on the video was himself. Wisely, he admitted the person on film looked like him but that it also looked like a number of other people and pleaded that we had the wrong man. The interrogator began to doubt the video and the case against the person. In effect, he doubted himself and worried that he might help convict an innocent man. Of course, no one wants to do that. The interrogator actually turned to the side of the suspect and became an advocate for his release. By developing additional physical evidence we were able to show the suspect was lying and eventually convince the suspect to reveal the true story.

For screeners and interrogators, mostly young and inexperienced, these are lessons they might never learn without competent guidance. Combat experience has a way of bloating one's confidence that in a few months you have seen it all. In other words, a young interrogator with a tour in Iraq inflates his opinion of his ability. There is still no better substitute than years of varied experience tempered with mature judgment. My experience in Iraq confirmed that in general, both experience and judgment were in short supply. Immaturity manifests itself in other problems related to poor judgment. I remember a 26-year-old military intelligence sergeant asking me to allow his Iraqi girlfriend access to the base. He was able to get her a job on base and didn't think she should have to go through security screening, that his judgment was good enough to vouch for her. He may have even tried to impress her with his authority by promising she would not have to submit to screening. When I informed him that his judgment was clouded with infatuation and that ALL persons with access to the base had to be screened by an independent third party he became indignant. He insisted that his five years experience in the Army should be honored. After all, he worked in intelligence too and could tell the good guys from the bad guys. The thought of an NCO even posing such a scenario sent red flags soaring as to the training and ethics we were teaching our young soldiers. Let me caveat that statement with praise for our military, of which I was a part, but such praise should never preclude valid criticism designed to help improve.

Another small but useful advantage is the threat of captivity. In one sense, interrogation is about control. If an interrogator can control all aspects of a suspect's environment it produces a powerful motivation for the suspect to cooperate. Establishing the notion of control begins at the minute of capture. Simply being restrained can create enough fear in a suspect's mind of the seriousness of the situation to gain cooperation. Actual captivity can create even more strain on the person, providing leverage to the interrogator. For those untrained to resist interrogation it takes little time for captivity to have a psychological effect. Simple shepherds turned insurgents have little experience with actual captivity but have heard the horror stories. When first captured they are frightened and can more easily be manipulated. That effect wears off however, as a suspect adjusts to captivity. Many have been told the European line that America is the world's biggest bully but when they meet Americans they quickly learn to appreciate American friendliness and concern for others. When they receive medical care, hot food, and good treatment the fear of imprisonment fades. A good interrogator takes maximum advantage of the initial shock of captivity if he senses the suspect is susceptible to the effect. The window of advantage can last anywhere from a few hours to no more than a few days depending on the conditions.

However, those insurgents trained to resist interrogation require more sophisticated approaches. Of course, rapport building is the one most often mentioned by law enforcement or strategic interrogators and it can be quite effective but it takes time. An appropriate example involves the FBI interrogation of Saddam Hussein by Special Agent George Piro, who explained his story on the "60 Minutes" television show. Saddam's environment remained completely controlled by the interrogator. Every aspect of Saddam's life including food, paper & pencil, toilet paper, even knowledge of the time of day was carefully controlled. Over seven months Piro built a relationship of dependency that evolved into cooperation. No coercive techniques were ever employed and would not likely have worked with Saddam. Patient psychological approaches slowly took effect. Once again, such methods require time, which is often a luxury in war. There is a place for rapport building in interrogation and a time compressed version can be applied in the field but it is not a panacea.

Battlefield interrogation faces time limits and perishable intelligence. For someone trained to resist, or under pressing time constraints, breaking a suspect's will quickly can require more harsh methods or more cunning ruses. A suspect can often resist the pressure of interrogation himself but weakens with the thought of his family or loved ones under interrogation. I want the reader to consider scenarios of this sort of which there are many.

Let's say a suspect is in custody and refuses to cooperate. He has been captured before by local forces and has endured harsh physical treatment so will not respond to such an approach or threat of it. But let's say we bring in his mother and tell him that she will be subjected to harsh treatment (even though she will not). He continues to resist but is weakening. Secretly we tell the mother that her son has undergone harsh treatment but refuses to cooperate with us. We tell the mother that there is one chance to save her son. We ask her to plead with him to cooperate, informing her she will have only 15 seconds so she must be convincing. We even tell her what to say. She agrees. We place her into a room opposite of her son where the walls are thin plywood, so he can hear his mother but not see her. On our cue, the mother calls to her son in anguish crying, "Oh son, I cannot take this anymore, please tell them what they want to know. Please help your mother." The son breaks down, screaming for his mother but she is taken away crying. He decides to cooperate, providing verifiable information to the interrogators.

In this scenario, no one was actually caused any physical harm but each side believed the other side was in severe physical pain. Because each side believed, the effect was the same as if physical force had been used. Does such a scenario constitute torture? Should it be prohibited? There are those who would argue that it rises to the level of torture, based on the emotional trauma caused to both parties in convincing them that physical harm had been done to the other.

In another scenario we need not use a relative. As I said, the fear of physical harm can be more powerful than actual harm. In this scenario, a suspect is resisting conventional means of interrogation. We hood him and convince him he is being transported to a secret interrogation center where the methods are less friendly. We drive him around the base a little and bring him back to a special dimly lit damp room. As he enters, we remove the hood and just before he sits down, we throw a bucket of water over some red liquid on the floor that looks like blood, washing it into a drain. "Next," I motion to the prisoner and he is handcuffed to the chair. In the next room is another prisoner. I tell the guard I have to finish next door and to wait here with the prisoner. Beyond the thin walls in the next room is one of our Arab interpreters who will act as a prisoner. As we begin questioning we occasionally connect two live wires to produce an electric shock sound loud enough for the prisoner to hear while the interpreter lets out screams of pain and Arabic pleas for mercy. I pretend to crank up the electricity to the point that the lights in the prisoner's room flicker with the electric shocks. After a few minutes the interpreter pretends to confess and the mock interrogation is stopped. I now return to the room with the prisoner who is sufficiently frightened. I begin questioning, "Look,

I know you don't believe me but this is a difficult job. I don't like to do these things but they are required if you do not cooperate. If you cooperate now you will save us all a lot of trouble." The prisoner begins to reveal verifiable information we need to know.

Now, does this ruse constitute torture? Obviously, no one was physically hurt but sufficient fear was created to induce cooperation. Should this type of technique be prohibited? Again, there are those who would argue that it should. My point is, based on the assessed vulnerabilities of a suspect, we can construct infinite scenarios to induce sufficient fear to cooperate. What if in the above scenario the suspect still refuses to cooperate, what then? The interrogator will lose credibility if he does not follow through. I say no. The interrogator already admitted he did not want to administer these techniques. He could move into conventional interrogation methods and slowly increase the pressure using stress positions or other ruses. The effectiveness depends on the skills of the interrogator to assess the suspect's weaknesses and the interrogator's ability to be convincing in his approach.

Hooding, isolation, loud music, varying temperatures, sleep deprivation, stress positions, attention grabs, threats and fear are all methods that can work when administered in proper measure and with proper skill. Limitations can be crafted to allow them to be administered safely; however, if the options are taken away by policymakers, then severe handicap is placed on interrogators' ability to gather information in a timely manner.

8   Mosul

Having spent part of my tour in Iraq at the now most famous prison in the world, Abu Ghraib, I transferred to one of Iraq's hot spots at that time, Mosul. I remember clearly my early impression of the area.

As I drove home along the potholed dirt road that ringed the Mosul airfield, enemy mortar rounds flew far over my head impacting with a distinctive concussion, boom-boom, boom-boom, four, no five sets of double booms, creating a strange light to my right, a splash of fire and sparks. I drove faster to exit the line of fire as quickly as possible, feeling a slight tension in my body reminding me of the urgency. Before reaching the end of the wrap-around road, an emergency vehicle shouldered cars to the side, red and blue lights flashing but no siren, as it raced to the impact area. Uh-oh, I thought, this time the mortars met their intended targets. Who could it be? Was my room hit, the chow hall teeming with hungry GIs at dinner or the gym, catching "Joe" in his shorts and t-shirt? The night moved forward and I forgot it all. After reading a little I dozed off. Rat-tat-tat-tat-tat, the unmistakable sound of machine guns, followed by a whoosh and explosion roused me from a sound sleep. Defying orders, I jumped to the window with blurry eyes, the sound of helicopters finally piercing my dreary brain. Two or three circled overhead searching for a target. Rat-tat-tat-tat-tat, they shot again into the city of over one million people with tracer bullets drawing a clear line to the earth below. Rockets followed the machine guns with a roman candle-like glow, as they streak toward some unfortunate insurgent on the ground. Hopefully, an innocent is not at the other end of those booms, I thought. Checking my watch, it is 10:26 pm. Whirling around again the silhouette of several choppers appeared against the faint moonlit sky. More machine guns, more rockets into the city. The GIs who had stopped momentarily to watch the show now returned to their private lives. Some never bothered to interrupt their video games or DVD watching. As for me, I longed to be in the chopper firing down on the enemy. Instead, I am doomed merely to watch the action like a common spectator. Not everyone gets to pull the triggers, some drive trucks, some order supplies, some guard gates, others gather intelligence or interrogate prisoners trying to discover where the insurgents hide or where they will strike next. I think I would rather pull the triggers. The next morning I learned that four U.S. persons, including one contractor, were injured by the mortars. Welcome to Mosul.

The larger city of Mosul encompasses what was once the ancient Biblical city of Nineveh, where the prophet Jonah preached and eventually convinced the king and its citizens to repent. His tomb still towers over parts of the city. Nineveh once served as the proud capital of the Assyrian Empire, which had stretched from Egypt and present day Turkey in the West, to present day Iran in the East. For centuries, this crossroad city has been inhabited by Babylonians, Medes, Christians and Muslims, Arabs and Kurds, Assyrians, Yezidis and Turkomans. Mosul built up around Nineveh. The word *Mosul* is said to be Arabic for "linking point" and in essence it joined the eastern trade routes from India with the West. The city grew in importance under the Persians and rose to become the capital of Mesopotamia in the 8th century, only to be once again destroyed by the Mongols in the 1200s. Strategic location helped it rise again under the Ottoman Empire and this city on the Tigris prospered even under Saddam. At one time, the University of Mosul claimed the largest education and research center in the Middle East.

Where once sat a prosperous city of antiquity, now I saw the shell of a third world disaster. If there were any nice parts left of Mosul, I didn't see them. I viewed more of the city by air than from the ground, but scarred by war and neglect it seemed pretty run down, the Biblical section of Nineveh overrun with squatters and reduced to a small remnant of the sprawling city grown up around it. U.S. military personnel generally did not venture there, and there was no reason to other than for tourism and our forces weren't in Mosul to see the sights. Having said that, a number of us still wanted to visit the ancient part of the city. To travel this close and not be able to visit an historic site such as Nineveh seemed a tragedy. But security precluded traveling within Mosul except when absolutely necessary.

Soon after arriving, I realized how complex the security problem had become. By late 2004, Mosul had become a lawless area. On the north side of the city sat Camp Courage later renamed Camp Freedom. The U.S. Army carved out a small base by commandeering Saddam's palace compound and transforming it into the headquarters of Task Force Freedom (TFF). Due south of Freedom sat Marez, which is either one base or two depending on how you look at it. The military unit in charge before I arrived managed it as two bases, Mosul Air Field (MAF) and Marez. The two bases consisted of more than 6,000 acres containing about 4,000 troops. MAF contained most of the support activities including a recreation center, tent gym, DFAC, containerized housing units, and of course the air field. Marez held more operational units, the DFAC that the suicide bomber blew up, and limited support facilities for the troops. Sugar Beet Road, a two lane boulevard, separated the two bases. Once an active Iraqi highway, had it not been almost totally closed to traffic, the two bases surely would have been considered one. But Sugar Beet was a main thoroughfare in Mosul that could not be completely closed to traffic without detouring travelers miles out of their way and the military command authorities deemed that impractical. So the U.S. military kept the road open but restricted traffic between Marez &

MAF with checkpoints and obstacles to ensure security of the bases on either side of it.

The U.S. military unit, which arrived about the same time as me, the 2/180 Field Artillery (Forward), brought with it an outstanding command staff of officers and enlisted. They administered the two bases as one, which proved a much wiser management decision. Size presented only part of the security problem. You can imagine that a base of 6,000 acres has a long perimeter that must be defended 24 hours a day. Scores of towers spaced at strategic intervals and manned by soldiers of Peshmerga (Kurdish Freedom Fighters) kept a watchful eye for insurgents or activity in the city which in some places butted right up against the fence or in other places, a concrete block wall. Howeer, the larger problem involved the foreign national workers allowed access to both Marez & MAF. Thousands of workers visited or lived on the base. Some workers performed labor and others translated; a large number of workers operated shops for the soldiers to buy jewelry and crafts. Still others opened restaurants, barbershops and internet cafes. Some workers came from the local community, others from much further away, in order to obtain a job. We employed Iraqi Arabs, Kurds, Turkmen, Iranians, Turks, contract workers from the Philippines, Pakistan, India, Nepal, Somalia and several other countries. The crux of the problem when I arrived revolved around the fact that we did not know how many foreigners worked on the base. We estimated several thousand but no one knew for sure.

Each military unit sponsored foreign nationals and were responsible for their conduct but the system left much to be desired including huge security vulnerabilities. Over 90 military units and several other entities connected to the U.S. Embassy operated on base, several of which existed in their own feudal, physically separated areas. Special Forces, for example, lived in a compound within a compound, inaccessible to most personnel of the base. Our first task became how to wrap our arms around the foreign national population ultimately accounting for every person with access to the base. Step two involved screening these individuals to determine if any were known "bad guys" or if any had been part of the Saddam regime even remotely. The U.S. military had created a screening process which entailed fingerprinting, photographing and interviewing each person, running their names through a half-baked database that included spotty criminal records, incomplete military records and partial Baath Party records from the former regime. This process was hastily thrown together after the Marez bombing in 2004 and bases all over Iraq were forced to implement it as a CYA to ensure there were no repeats of the DFAC bombing.

While well intentioned, the system posed numerous problems. Few people were properly trained to perform the interviews. A protocol was written to guide the screening operations known as the Personnel Screening Standard Operating Procedure. Unfortunately, a large number of those conducting the screening interviews showed disregard for the process or basic ignorance of it. I remember several screeners who did not even know such an SOP (Standard Operating Procedure) existed, yet they were making critical judgments on whether foreign nationals should be authorized access. Among screeners, clear standards were lacking and the standards provided were enforced differently at different locations. The computer system used to track those screened personnel was known as BATS, an acronym for Biometric Analytical Tool Set. I was told the government bought the system for hundreds of millions of dollars and once again the taxpayers were bilked. BATS included a database purported to include huge files of data, fingerprints, photos and even eye scans to precisely identify Iraqis. Such a system was needed as the Iraqi national ID card was almost useless. Americans, used to accepting without question American IDs, assumed the same standards existed in Iraq. Unfortunately, cards were easily forged and could be purchased in the market for a few Dinars. After the fall of Saddam, thousands of Iraqis changed their identity, some to obscure previous positions in the regime, others to cover past criminal records. In theory, had it worked well, a system like BATS filled a niche sorely needed by U.S. Forces. Thousands of local national employees worked for the military throughout Iraq. It became critical to know who we hired, if they had ever been arrested by civilian authorities or Coalition Forces, or if they had been previous members of the Baath Party loyal to Saddam. We also needed to track employees fired or barred from U.S. installations. It is hard to imagine the number of thieves, cheats, rapists, con men, gang members, men trying to avoid the law in other places, troublemakers and assorted crooks banned from military installations not to mention insurgents, those suspected of providing intelligence to the insurgency, or intelligence agents of Turkey or Iraq. A person fired from one base in southern Iraq would just move to another part of the country and find himself quickly hired again by an unwitting unit. In fact, we discovered Iraqis fired from Camp Courage on the other side of Mosul who showed up working on our post just a few miles away. The military needed a reliable system providing everyone access to background information on local nationals, especially derogatory information. I was told that after the U.S. military left Iraq, the entire BATS system would be given to the Iraqi government.

Sadly, the system purchased was a failure. First, it could not handle the overwhelming data collected on each person. By 2005, there were well over 100,000 Iraqis in the database with the number climbing daily. Local nationals turned over quickly, some only working for a few days. Initially, poorly trained military and civilian contractors input data haphazardly or created incomplete files. More troubling, we later discovered that data had been lost or corrupted so the system did not alert on persons that it should have. It became a joke among screeners who would input their own fingerprints or photos and then test the system to see if BATS would detect them. I don't remember a time when it actually passed that test. Much worse, BATS could not even correctly identify people in the system by name much of the time, producing dangerously inconsistent results. The system was supposed to automatically check for similar spellings of a name. As I mentioned earlier, there are more ways to spell Mohammed than you imagine: Muhammed, Mahammed, Mohammad, Mohamed, Muhamed, and several more. In addition, names might be reversed to fool screeners. Mohammed Ahmed Ali might be changed to Ahmed Ali Mohammed or Ali Ahmed Mohammed. If you throw in a few spelling derivations, a person's previous record could easily remain undetected. If we were suspicious we would plug in derivations manually and often times discover the system had failed us. I am not suggesting that all of the derivations were intentional. Persons entering data might mistakenly input incorrect information, or the data may have even been collected poorly. Screeners relied on interpreters of varying ability and motivation. Whatever spelling they recommended was often the one entered into the computer. I was shocked to learn how many Americans and worse yet, their interpreters confused family name and given names. As mentioned earlier, the Arab system of naming posed its own complexity. Mohammed Ahmed Ali's son would traditionally take the first name of his father and grandfather so the son might become Khalid Mohammed Ahmed and Khalid's son Salim would become Salim Khalid Mohammed. Such a system increased the difficulty for Americans to track local family relationships.

Completely trusting a system that did not work 100% of the time lulled some U.S. personnel into a false sense of security. We only began to discover the defects when our own corporate memories caused us to question the BATS output. All too frequently, a foreign national would appear for interview and one of us would remember interviewing him months before but no data would emerge from BATS inquiries. Or during an interview, the person would admit having been processed several times in the past but BATS failed to produce a record of it. However, we worked with what we had knowing the military was not about to ditch this horse in midstream. We dutifully continued to input data into BATS knowing much of it would disappear; causing us to routinely use BATS but never completely rely on it. If the information we needed appeared, we used it, but if it did not appear and we had suspicions, then we pursued other methods of inquiry.

A chronic problem within the military system was the lack of follow-up. Matters routinely fell through the cracks because they were rarely pursued to the end and closed out properly. Individuals assumed someone else would take care of it. A screener assumes a foreign national was properly entered into BATS and does not check for certain. A subordinate sends a message to higher headquarters informing them of a problem and never follows up to see what was done to correct it, and so it is forgotten and never corrected. I believe the main cause of this problem was the "stay in your lane" mentality. Despite the "Army of One" slogan most subordinates were afraid to step outside the strict boundaries of their responsibility for fear of sharp rebuke to "stay in your lane." This fostered an environment where issues fell through the cracks because one side assumed someone else was handling it. Individuals only ensured that they covered themselves. A sergeant says, "I reported that a military gate guard is allowing an Iraqi interpreter to check IDs of locals, which is improper, but I won't check to see if anyone actually corrected the problem because I passed it off, it's not my lane." So, unauthorized activity might continue because someone didn't follow-up. You encounter countless examples every day but are powerless to change the macro "stay in your lane" mentality that pervades the military.

9   Foreign Contract Workers

In northern Iraq, thousands of Turkish workers filled the needs of the U.S. military. Under contract with Turkish companies for construction, transportation, supplies and a host of other services, the Turkish village on MAF and Marez grew almost as large as the American. In general, Turks are good, hard working people. Politically and economically, the U.S. benefited from employing them on its bases. Turks collected the trash, cooked food in the DFAC, built concrete barriers, hauled gravel, cleared roads, and all manner of low to high skilled labor for considerably less cost than U.S. workers could have performed those tasks. In addition, the Turks proved far less of a security risk than Iraqi workers, because Turkey is a staunch ally, not involved in the insurgency, at least not directly. The relationship worked well for Turkey too. At the time its economy was sagging and the employment in Iraq provided jobs for idle workers, whose income in turn, helped Turkey recover in its own small way. Not all the Turks worked under contract, a number were entrepreneurs who received permission to start businesses on post. Before long, dozens of stores opened including jewelry shops, luggage stores, handicrafts, tailors, carpet stores, barbershops, and a group of restaurants and kabob stands. Soldiers denied the opportunity to shop in town, with pockets full of money and nowhere to spend it welcomed the small businesses.

Inevitably, however, problems arose with some of the Turks. It turned out that the main contractors recruited most of their workers from Adana. Apparently, the local economy there was on the skids providing ready labor for duty in Iraq. Local businesses, some of which were located outside a U.S. Air Force base that had downsized, sought new opportunities in Iraq. Unfortunately, more than a few of the thousands that decided to make the move to Iraq were unsavory characters. Men in trouble with the law signed up for duty to escape difficulty in Adana. Some of the small-time Turkish mafia that controlled the slumping businesses in Adana also moved to Iraq and eventually tried to control the business in Mosul on U.S. military installations. We did not realize the internal struggle until reports from shop employees began to filter in about the beatings and intimidation. I remember one older man literally crying that he did not know what to do after his Turkish boss had beaten him several times and threatened to kill him. The employee did not want us to ban the Turkish boss, concerned that the employee and his family would eventually face worse treatment upon returning to Turkey. Another Turk operated a kind of extortion ring, lending money to several businessmen to open establishments on military bases in Iraq. He arranged sponsors for them among the military units whom he had befriended and then collected monthly amounts from the owners after they established themselves on base. Sometimes he got a little rough with the businessmen who weren't making as much as he had planned. Finally, a member of the command politely informed the Turk that if he didn't stop we would ban him from all bases in Iraq. It may have drove his activities deeper undercover but we didn't see any more black & blue Turks around base for a while.

With the number of Turks in the thousands, we could also expect that drugs and weapons would soon appear on base. Both presented bad news for U.S. Forces. Where there are drugs, violence follows and Command wanted none of it. We nipped both in the bud at the slightest hint.

One day, Force Protection brought in a Turkish laborer suspected of connections to illegal weapons on base. We really had no evidence, only the word of another worker. It was entirely possible the worker informing on the Turk either wanted to eliminate a rival, avenge some wrong done to him or endear himself to us in order to ask special favors. The man who was escorted in, Savas, appeared thin and frail. He seemed meek, almost effeminate, not the stereotype of a weapons trafficker. During the routine screening questions used to establish rapport we broached the subject of weapons on base. He squirmed at the thought, posting initial obligatory denials. His non-verbals, however, cried out that he was hiding something most likely out of fear.

After more than an hour he finally admitted knowing one man who had a weapon but the timid Turk feared revealing the man's name because of certain retribution either here or back in Turkey. "There might be one man with a weapon but he is feared among the workers," Savas doodled with his finger on top of the table.

"Are you afraid of this man?" I asked hoping to keep the conversation going before his hint of courage ran out.

"He is tall and mean, and some say he has a gun. Even for saying this much I could be in danger." With this Savas lifted his head and looked straight at me searching for reassurance.

"Listen to me Savas, we will protect your identity. No one will know how we discovered the information. I am only trying to prevent an incident that might cause injury or death. A weapon on this base is a danger to all of us." He shook his head in agreement. "Have you ever seen the gun?" I continued to prod resisting the temptation to force Savas to actually name him until he was ready.

"Yes, sometimes he brandishes it to scare us. He has connections to the Turkish mafia," he said.

I nodded and raising my eyebrows to show interest asked, "Did he ever mention why he needs a gun here?"

"Two reasons," he said. "First of all, he needed the gun to keep others in line. Having the weapon demonstrated his power. Secondly, he mentioned that he expected trouble upon returning to Turkey this summer and wanted the gun handy." Savas had revealed much knowledge and was now too deep to refuse naming him. Once again I promised to protect him but pressed to know his name. Finally, Savas straightened himself in the chair gathering the courage to speak the name. "Osman is his name."

"Thank you," I said. "Where does Osman live?"

Looking away from me Savas pursed his lips before speaking, "He stays on the Airfield side in building C, room 102, the same corridor as me. You promised to protect me. He is a violent man and as you can see I am not a man of great strength."

Leaning forward to show my sincerity I replied, "I will keep my promise. When was the last time you saw the handgun?"

"He had it as recently as last night but I do not know where he stores it," he said.

I slipped a note to my partner to quickly search the records to find out if we could verify the information on Osman. I turned back to continue questioning Savas, "Did he ever say where he got it or how he managed to sneak it in the country?"

Savas searched his mind and then continued, "Adil, a kitchen worker, brought it into the country on our company airplane. Adil boasts that he can smuggle anything into or out of the country right under the nose of the U.S. military."

With only a short investigation we verified that Osman in fact worked for a Turkish company on base and verified his dormitory room. We also verified that Adil was out of the country on home leave and would not return for several months.

We quickly obtained the Base Commander's permission to search Osman's room. Force Protection and I assembled a raid team and set out for the dorms on the other side of the runway that evening. Housing for the Turks was mostly separated from the U.S. soldiers and U.S. personnel were prohibited from visiting the Turkish area to prevent fraternization and possible trouble. As CI agents on official duty we often accepted invitations to eat in the Turkish cafeteria with local officials. Turkish food prepared for the workers was simple and nutritious, always served with fresh baked bread, which I loved. Killing two birds with one stone, whenever I ate in the Turkish cafeteria, I frequently made a point to tour the living area just in case we needed to raid it in the future. This was one of those occasions.

Soldiers loved to conduct raids, which offered a kind of excitement not normally part of routine patrols and daily activity. After a planning and strategy briefing, we piled into the Humvees and headed across the base to MAF Airfield. Just after dark, four military vehicles came to an abrupt halt in front of the Turkish dorms and Force Protection soldiers jumped out fully armed and prepared for a fight though not provoking one. The Turks lived in prefabricated, one story metal buildings on concrete slabs. Luckily for us, Osman happened to live in the second room inside the main entrance to dormitory "A." Two soldiers entered the dorm and knocked on Osman's door. No sooner than his roommate cracked opened the door the soldiers rushed in demanding all in the room down on the floor. As soon as the others in the building realized we were conducting a raid, contraband started flying out all the windows in the building. Occupants threw cell phones, knives, porn magazines, and prohibited electronic devices out the windows, it seemed all at once. At first I was startled but when it dawned on me I chuckled. The Turks knew that if they were caught with any of these items they could lose their jobs and be sent home. What they did not know was that we were not conducting a full search of the dorm looking for contraband; we had a specific mission. Two Force Protection soldiers began collecting the contraband items from the ground as I returned to the front of the building.

One by one the soldiers brought out the roommates and I directed them separated and guarded to ensure they could not communicate with each other. While two soldiers began searching the small, approximately eight by eight foot room containing four people's belongings, we began field questioning the roommates. Two of the roommates were new to Iraq, arriving within the past week and genuinely appeared ignorant of Osman or his activities. The third roommate had returned to Turkey a week earlier so he remained out of our reach for the time being. Force Protection was drawing a blank in its search so I took Osman away from the building for direct questioning. I could plainly see his nervousness. In the pitch dark I under lit my face with a small flashlight so the shadows looked a bit scary, kind of like kids do at Halloween. I stood face to face with Osman and told him in a stern voice that he knew why we were there. At this point, we only wanted the weapon. If he cooperated, we would be lenient. If we found the weapon before he confessed, things would turn bad for him. He said he only wanted to return to Turkey. I advised him that if he produced the weapon he would be on a convoy out of Iraq that evening. Osman confessed the handgun was hidden inside one of the speaker boxes of his stereo. We literally had to disassemble the speakers to find it, cleverly concealed securely inside the box and wrapped in dark foil. We escorted him and a few others back to the office for follow-up questioning, corroborating additional information he provided about where he obtained the weapon and what he planned to do with it. Force Protection OIC, Major White, quickly ordered him off the FOB, placing Osman on the next convoy to the Turkish border leaving late that night. We learned significant intelligence about Turkish mafia among the workers which would later prove valuable when we discovered potential connections of Turkish criminals to insurgents.

Not realizing it until late in our tour, cooperation between Al Qaeda and Turkish criminal elements presented a serious vulnerability. Running low on operating cash, Al Qaeda elements at some point began concocting creative ways to raise money. One way was to kidnap foreigners and hold them for ransom, which made Turks more vulnerable because they were plentiful and the larger companies would pay handsomely for the return of key employees.

10 THE KIDNAPPING OF FATIH

I didn't come to know Fatih until after his ordeal. Major White, Force Protection OIC knew him first. He described Fatih's story as he remembered it:

> The first time I heard Fatih's name was just after I arrived in Iraq in late January 2005. As I was getting to know the base, the people living there and all the issues, I kept hearing bits and pieces of a story about a young guy who had worked here and had been kidnapped by insurgents the previous November. As people started to know me better they began revealing more about what had occurred on base. After a couple of weeks, an employee of KBR security filled me in on what he knew, explaining that Fatih was a Turk and had originally come to Iraq with his father to work for KBR. Not long after Fatih arrived, he decided to open his own store selling t-shirts and other items to soldiers. Sometime in November, no one knew the exact date, Fatih was kidnapped off of the FOB and had not been seen since.

The KBR employee told me that he tried talking to other soldiers about the kidnapping but no one would listen because Fatih was Turkish and considered just another victim of war. I asked the KBR employee why this would concern me and he explained of rumors that FPS (Facilities Protection Service) workers assisted in the kidnapping and some still worked on the base. At the time, FPS workers were local Iraqis hired to help guard the base and man the gates. Since the DFAC bombing in December, almost all of the Iraqi's had left or been fired and replaced by Kurdish (KDP) and PUK soldiers. I asked the employee to find out more details and keep me informed. About a week later, the KBR employee brought Fatih's father to visit me for what turned out to be an interesting conversation. A kind, soft-spoken old gentleman, Fatih's father confided that his son was kidnapped around the end of November and when he tried telling officers in the military unit in charge, at the time, they did not listen. I assured him I would listen and asked him to tell me everything he knew. Happy to finally find a friendly ear, the elderly gentlemen told me that the day of his kidnapping Fatih had said that he was going to take a taxi to Mosul to buy items to sell in his store on the base. Dad learned that Fatih had gone to Alpha Gate, which had since been closed, and waited for the taxi. When it didn't arrive, he accepted a ride from an FPS worker at the gate and that was the last time anyone saw him.

Dad started looking for Fatih about two days later but could not find him. He tried telling the soldiers about Fatih, but no one seemed to care. As he questioned people to find out what happened to his son, he started hearing rumors of a suicide bomb to be set off on the FOB. Dad told the American soldiers in charge about it but again they would not listen. U.S. military officers told dad he did not know what he was talking about and that no one could smuggle a bomb on the base—how wrong they were! According to dad, rumors about the bombing became so detailed that locals stopped coming to work on the base and foreign workers asked to be sent home. Ironically, dad insisted it seemed that everyone but the American soldiers knew there would be a bombing.

Dad continued trying to find his son and talked to anyone that would listen but no one would talk or listen. Not until December 21st, when 22 people lost their lives and more than 60 were wounded did anyone take notice. A couple of days later, a few soldiers finally asked the old man to explain what he knew.

After relating the entire story to the soldiers they concluded that his son was most likely dead. As a father he refused to accept this and held out hope for his son. He had heard that the insurgents were posting videos on the internet of those persons in custody, sometimes broadcasting their actual beheading. Everyday dad checked these sites until one day, he saw Fatih on his knees with a knife to his throat. An insurgent speaking on the video threatened to cut off Fatih's head for working with the Americans. Hysterical, dad did not know exactly what to do but found comfort in knowing his son was still alive.

Around the end of December, he received a call on his cell phone from the insurgents holding Fatih captive, threatening that if he did not pay $15,000, they would cut off Fatih's head and send it to him. With the help of friends, and scraping together all the family savings, he managed to come up with enough money. Arrangements were made for payment and the money was delivered around mid-January to the insurgents. Dad asked that Fatih be released close to the base but the insurgents refused and for a while he did not know if Fatih had been released or killed. I asked the father if he still had anyone he could contact, to find out what happened to his son and he broke down crying that he tried everyone he knew but no one could help. Dad said he even called the insurgents but they had stopped answering the phone. I told dad that there was not much I could do for him at that time since no one knew where Fatih was, but that if his son resurfaced I would help any way I could and wanted to talk to Fatih personally.

Well, I did not have to wait long. Around mid-February the KBR employee returned to see me with news that Fatih was alive. He learned that after the insurgents collected the money they drove Fatih north into the green zone. The northern green zone starts about 30 kilometers north of Mosul and stretches to the Turkish & Iranian border. This is a safe area for Kurds and Americans. If an Iraqi or Turkish person is found in this area they will be killed on sight! Remember Fatih is Turkish. The father had learned that Fatih had been released about 10 kilometers south of Dohuk, which is a Kurdish city in northern Iraq within the green zone. The insurgents kept Fatih's passport and all of his papers and told him to walk back to Turkey and never return. Dad knew all this because Fatih had called his family back in Turkey asking for help. Amazingly, Fatih had somehow walked all the way to Dohuk. As he was trying to find a ride from Dohuk up to the border, the PUK picked him up and were holding him in jail. PUK soldiers had interrogated Fatih and concluded he was a lying spy, demanding Fatih prove he was telling the truth or they would kill him. One of Fatih's last requests was to call his family who then called dad and told him of Fatih's situation. Dad asked if there was anyway I could help and I told him there was and I would.

Remember the PUK soldiers had replaced the Iraqis who helped guard the base, so I went to see the PUK Colonel in charge of the troops here. I told the Colonel Fatih's story and asked him to bring Fatih to Mosul so I could talk to him. The Colonel agreed to look into it and if Fatih was being held in Dohuk by the PUK he would have him released. About one week later the employee from KBR came to see me and told me Fatih had been released by the PUK and was now in Turkey. This was good for Fatih but bad for me because I could not interview Fatih, and I wanted to do so in person. I asked Fatih's father to convince Fatih to return to Mosul so I could find out what happened to him in detail. He confided that Fatih wanted to return but the Turkish government would not issue Fatih another passport or visa until they knew what happened. I offered to make some calls and see what I could do.

Able to contact a few people that could assist Fatih's family in this matter, I explained what had happened and asked if they could help to clear things up for Fatih. A week later dad came to see me happy that Fatih had his passport and visa but no transportation to Iraq. The family had spent all of its money on the ransom and was now completely broke. Again, I offered to help, deciding to contact the president of a Turkish company working on post. Fatih used to work for that particular company and they liked him and seemed glad to assist. After a pleasant conversation with a company official he agreed the company would arrange transportation for Fatih from Turkey to Mosul, via one of the regularly scheduled flights from Turkey to Iraq, which carried their employees to and fro.

After much effort, Fatih arrived back in Mosul around the end of February and it felt really good to see Fatih and his father together again. Fatih's dad pledged he would do anything for me in thanks for what I had done, but I insisted he did not owe me anything, that I also had a son and understood what he went through. When I was finally able to sit down and talk to Fatih, he told a truly amazing story. Fatih described how on November 21st he went to Alpha gate intending to take a taxi to Mosul for some shopping. Fatih called a friend named Ali and asked Ali to have his dad, a taxi driver, come pick him up. Fatih said he did not trust anyone else because of all the kidnappings and killings going on at that time. As Fatih waited at the gate he started talking to four FPS workers on guard duty there with the American soldiers. One of these workers was Ahmed a friend of Fatih's from Turkey, who grew up in the same village. As they were talking, Fatih mentioned he was waiting for a taxi. One of the FPS guards said there was no need to wait and offered to take him in his car. Fatih politely refused, deciding to wait for Ali's dad. A short time later Fatih called Ali and found out his dad was caught in traffic and did not know when he would arrive.

Fatih told the FPS workers his ride would arrive late and the same Iraqi again offered Fatih a ride. To his later regret, Fatih decided to accept the ride and they both got in to the FPS worker's blue Opal. As they drove out the gate, the Iraqi turned left instead of right, heading towards Baghdad traffic circle. This traffic circle is away from downtown Mosul and had been the scene of numerous bombings and firefights. Startled, Fatih told the driver to turn back because he did not want to go that way. The man pulled out a pistol and jammed it in Fatih's ribs, laughing that they were going to meet the mujahadeen. Fatih did not want to believe the man was serious but when he looked behind he saw a black station wagon following them, the men inside wearing black headgear covering their faces like the mujahadeen. Fatih yelled to the man to drive faster but instead the man pulled over and stopped. When Fatih got out of the car and saw all the guns he was so scared he could not run. One of the insurgents ran up to Fatih and immediately punched him in the mouth knocking him to the ground. As Fatih lay there he saw the guy who offered him the ride shake hands with the insurgents and then drive off. They forced Fatih to lie on the floor of the car, their feet on top of him.

The insurgents drove to a house where Fatih was transferred to another car and taken to yet another place. At this new house, they shoved Fatih to the basement and chained his neck and hands to the wall. For a couple of days they did not speak to Fatih and only fed him once a day. Around the third day they brought in an 18-year old boy who had been badly beaten and chained him next to Fatih. The boy had been selling oil in the city in an area controlled by the insurgents. When they found out, they captured him, beat him and brought him to the safe house.

Over the next several days, five or six more men were brought down to the basement and imprisoned in the adjoining rooms. When the guards left, the captives would talk and find out each other's identity. Fatih said there were Turks, Iraqis, and other foreigners in the group. After about two weeks more insurgents came and announced that they were going to kill all of them for working with the Americans. Fatih appealed to one of the insurgents who looked to be 20-22 years old and spoke perfect English. The insurgent appeared American at first, but when Fatih inquired, the man denied it, claiming instead that he was one of the people launching rockets and mortars at the base. The insurgent asked Fatih how many Americans he killed and Fatih told him none. The insurgent did not like this answer and proceeded to beat Fatih.

After about two more days they took Fatih and another captive into a room and told them Abu Al Zarqawi was coming to cut off their heads. Fatih broke down crying and begging for his life. Not long after, Zarqawi walked in and announced that Fatih would die for working with the Americans. Fatih said he begged for his life, reminding Zarqawi, "I am a Muslim from Turkey, you are Muslim from Iraq, we are brothers how can you kill me?" Fatih said Zarqawi pulled out a knife and said, "I will show you." Fatih continued to cry and beg for his life as they moved him to the wall. Fatih watched Zarqawi cut the head off of the other captive.

As they prepared Fatih for the same end, another insurgent walked in and advised Zarqawi not to kill Fatih because his father had agreed to pay a ransom. They decided to take Fatih back to his room and gave him food. The insurgents told Fatih that they did not want to do what they were doing but had to. Fatih said his captors treated him nicer after this but on several occasions they forced him to watch or listen to them kill other captives. He remarked that it is a haunting sound to hear the air leave a man's lungs when his head is being cut off.

After about another week they moved Fatih to a different house where an older man stood guard. This man seemed kind but had evil eyes and Fatih did not trust him. His captors kept Fatih at that location for about one week before unexpectedly placing him in the trunk of a BMW and announcing they were taking him home. They drove for about one hour and when the trunk finally opened, Fatih could see he was out in the middle of nowhere. Insurgents brusquely pointed Fatih north and told him to walk home.

Tired, confused and afraid, Fatih managed to walk to Dohuk before Kurdish Peshmerga picked him up and interrogated him about why he was in the area without any papers or identification. Fatih told them all that had happened but the Peshmerga remained unconvinced, at one point placing a gun to Fatih's head and calling him a liar to try and break him. They threatened to kill him for spying unless he proved he was telling the truth. At wits end, Fatih called his family and told them his situation but his family did not know what they could do to help him. The PUK decided to lock him in jail promising that he would die shortly. Surprisingly, about three days later the Kurds drove him to the Turkish border and released him. Fatih said he did not know why they did this but he was happy.

I told Fatih he could set up shop again on base and try to earn enough money to repay his family. Fatih thanked me and did just that, opening a t-shirt and carpet shop catering to customers who wanted unit jerseys or specialized imprints. In the meantime, I tried to convince military intelligence to question Fatih while he still held a wealth of knowledge fresh in his mind. Piecing together pieces of information from memory, Fatih was willing to show U.S. military intelligence the location of the insurgent safe houses. At that time there were still about a dozen foreigners held as hostages in Mosul and it would have been great just to free one of them. Fatih suffered through terrible nightmares long afterward because he was still afraid. To his credit, this tough, young Turk remained determined to find the insurgents responsible for the kidnappings and stop them. Fatih said he didn't care if he died in the process just as long as he could catch them, but no one in military intelligence seemed interested in exploiting his knowledge.

Fatih's case was not that uncommon. In June 2005, U.S. and Iraqi Forces rescued a 64-year old Australian contractor working in Iraq as an engineer. He had been taken hostage near Baghdad and unlike Fatih, a full-court diplomatic and religious press was orchestrated to secure his release. Others, whose names we may never know, were not so lucky.

11 TURKISH MAFIA ON BASE

Following the thousands of Turkish workers hired as subcontractors to U.S. Forces, financial opportunity in Iraq attracted seasoned Turkish criminals, some of whom were connected to Turkish organized crime which I will refer to as the Turkish Mafia. Almost as soon as Americans established military bases, Turks reacted quickly by setting up shops and restaurants that were well patronized by U.S. Forces. Within the safety of the perimeter, most of these people were good and mixed well with Americans. Mehmet had owned a Turkish kabob restaurant outside Incirlik Air Base in Turkey and decided to open a branch in Mosul. More than two decades of dealing with Americans made him well liked among the troops. One day I asked him why he liked working with Americans and he replied that, "Americans are mannerly and clean up after themselves. In Turkish restaurants they leave a mess. Americans don't. Americans are warm, friendly, and treat people well, they really understand human rights." I asked the same question to a 27-year old Turkish electrician, who replied, "Americans treat people well and if you work you get paid. In my country sometimes you work but don't get paid." I made it a point to ask workers if they thought America acted against Islam. One laborer surprised me with this answer, "America against Islam, certainly not. You have freedom of religion in your country. In Turkey, a newly elected female official was not allowed to enter parliament wearing her headscarf. That would never happen in America."

The troops needed a respite from the war zone and shopping at a Turkish jewelry store or eating kabobs at a Turkish restaurant was welcome by the soldiers. Entrepreneurial Turks even branched into the barber business opening several salons in different areas around the post. It is easy to underestimate the amount of money generated in these operations, as I did at first. To my utter surprise, I later learned that the jewelry shops alone could gross $20,000 per month and we had at least a half dozen of them spread across the two sides of the base. Hundreds of thousands of dollars were earned on our base alone each month by small shop owners. Turkish leaders were quite friendly and adept at endearing themselves to unit commanders who sponsored their access to the base. It wasn't long however until we found a criminal element developing among them. This was a small problem compared to our worry that once these criminal contacts were established in Iraq it would lead to Turkish criminals with unique access to the bases providing information to the insurgency. Since Turks kidnapped by the insurgency were worth money, it was only logical that Mafia elements might either supply names, support the kidnappings, translate for Iraqi insurgents, or make the necessary contacts in Turkey, all for a cut of the action.

Because units came to rely on their services and Turkish leaders were so friendly with unit officials, commanders tended to overlook a little unscrupulous behavior, a few even benefited from it. Most senior NCOs and commanders had no idea how much money these little mom and pop looking business were making. Frankly, they didn't care too much as long as the shop owners provided the services. One criminal family that began to dominate business on the base I will call the Giray family. Once Papa Giray had successfully established his barbershop and confection store it didn't take long until fifteen family members had arrived and received permission to open similar stores. Shop owners not part of the Giray ring were forced to pay extortion to remain in business. When Turkish workers, who had known the family in Turkey, began to report the Giray family's organized crime connections, few people believed them. Later, when threats to employees and severe beatings began to surface, we all began to take notice. The Turks were also largely responsible for one other irritant. Military General Order Number One strictly prohibited alcohol for the troops. Ostensibly, the rule was written to honor Muslim wishes and belay rumors that U.S. Forces would become a corrupting influence in the country. Privately, I think more senior level officers welcomed the rule as it certainly reduced the crime and alcohol related problems of the Vietnam era where alcohol reigned supreme. At any rate, the

Turks constantly smuggled liquor onto the base, mostly for their own consumption but not always. The regulation applied to them too but they had little regard for American rules.

Papa Giray was the big fish and we wanted to ban him from the base. However, he had wormed his way into the hearts of a few senior officers at TFF so unless we could prove either illegal activity or his mafia connections, he remained safe with the help of U.S. military top cover. A source, who had known Papa Giray in Turkey, told us of Papa's criminal past, including multiple felony convictions. As we often learned in our tour in Iraq, our own bureaucracy was our worst enemy. In this case, we tried to use our military contacts in Turkey to obtain a criminal background check on Papa Giray since he used to run several shops outside one of our military bases there. Everyone who had access to our bases underwent a criminal background check. Incredibly, our U.S. military contacts would not share information about Papa Giray because the Turkish government had instituted a rule that the government records Americans in Turkey had access to were not to be shared outside Turkey. I can understand our military not wanting to risk losing access to government records within Turkey, yet in this instance, it certainly would have been helpful if they slipped us something from his record quietly. Just think about this for a moment. Our U.S. military comrades in Turkey would not release known criminal information about a foreigner who could be a danger to U.S. troops in Iraq because they wanted to keep a promise to the Turkish government.

We had interviewed Papa Giray several times but he always insisted on his innocence. Without hard evidence we could not break him. The day finally came. Force Protection rolled up 17 Turks in a red access security badge violation ring. One of them was Papa Giray himself. He was running a ring smuggling workers onto the base, by taking red access badges of authorized employees, leaving the base and using those badges to escort unauthorized persons through the ID check at the gate. This was beyond criminal behavior; smuggling persons onto post presented a serious counterintelligence vulnerability. If Papa Giray could smuggle Turks on base he could also smuggle Iraqis and that meant insurgents could find their way in among us. Papa Giray insisted he was innocent, merely trying to bring in more workers to better man the shops serving the troops. That was an argument that served him well in the past. This time however, we wanted to nail the coffin shut on Papa.

He looked disheveled and out of his element when he sat down in the interrogation room. Now that I think about it, he looked a little like Saddam Hussein when he first crawled out of the rat hole in Tikrit. Papa's hair, usually well combed and oiled, was all mussed. He had not showered or shaved. His already rugged features and scarred face were now exaggerated in the dim light.

149

"Welcome my old friend," I said as he sat down. His English was near perfect and he detected my sarcasm.

"Help me," he begged, his hands cuffed together in front of him.

"Help you?" I echoed, "How can I help you when you won't help me?"

He countered quickly, "How can I help you? What have I done?"

Calmly I sat tapping the dossier on the table. "I have learned too late for you that you have been untruthful with me," I continued. I decided to combine two old law enforcement approaches the Army referred to as the File and Dossier and the "We Know All" techniques.

Wagging his head from side to side he answered, "How have I been untruthful? Tell me and I will correct this misunderstanding immediately." Papa knew he was in trouble this time and was trying to appear cooperative to curry favor.

"I am very disappointed in you Papa Giray. You may know that as the man in charge of security it is my responsibility to know everything that goes on within the base and to know all about the people living and working here." Papa nodded several times in agreement. "When I interviewed you in the past you told me you never had trouble with the law back in Turkey. I believed you. I trusted you. You have let me down severely. In fact, you have embarrassed me, tainted my credibility. This report from Turkey

150

has confirmed your deception." I waved the dossier several times and flung it on the desk for effect.

Giray slumped forward in his chair, acknowledging his previous lies through his body language. "Please understand that I never would cause you any harm but I was embarrassed about my past and did not want to give you the wrong impression about me. I am a good man who loves Americans."

"Yes, yes, that's what you said last time but now I know you are a liar. You lied about your past and you are lying now," I raised my voice to show my simmering impatience with him.

Giray leaned forward as he spoke. "How can I make it up to you? Tell me what the report says and I will clarify everything in it."

"No Giray, you tell me what the report says. I will judge your truthfulness for the last time. You know what you did wrong. Tell me each count in detail and I will know whether you are truthful," I said as I flipped through the imaginary report that was really just a collection of unrelated documents I threw together.

"I will, I will," he said. He sat back in the chair looking at the ceiling, recalling his background and deciding what to say next. Leaning forward again he began, "I am sure it speaks of my arrests for fighting. I have been arrested several times. Adana is a rough town. A man has to protect his territory." He smiles and raises his chin a little.

"C'mon Giray, you weren't just arrested for fighting," I appeared impatient with his partial answer.

"No, no well one of the fights ended up with the other man dead but it was just self defense." Giray pulled up his shirt to reveal a huge scar more that a foot long where he had been stabbed and sliced.

"Go on," I insisted, certain there was much more to confess.

"Well, it must say that I was convicted for possessing drugs, cocaine," he admitted.

Taking a chance I probed further. A man like Giray must have done more than possess drugs. "Possess you say?? Is that your final answer to me? And only one offense? I am losing my patience with you Giray."

"No, no," he confessed, "I had three convictions and one was for selling drugs. I admit it."

"Good, now we are getting somewhere Giray," I kept pressing until he reluctantly admitted arrests for several weapons violations. Suspecting he was still hiding something bigger. I took a chance and pressed him one final time. Shaking my head from side to side I tightened my jaws a little. "You have still held back the entire truth from me. Why should I waste my time with you? You cannot be trusted."

"What, what, show me the report and I will verify it. Maybe someone has made up lies about me. There is no more I swear it. I have told you everything!" he exclaimed.

Now, I began to worry that I had pushed too far. I had nothing but an investigator's instinct to know if anything remained unsaid. It was too late to back down now. But a man with his background must have something else, something bad that did not make it into a criminal record. It was too late to retreat from the bluff. I had to press it for all I could. I slid up closer to him and lowered my voice for effect. "Giray, not everything is... how we say... part of a criminal record. Some things are kept as notes. Documented but not prosecuted. You have not revealed it all. That's what I am so angry about."

Giray went silent, his head down in thought. Silence can be disturbing in interrogation. It may allow a suspect to think of an alibi. It can also allow him to gather the courage to become stubborn and stop cooperating. I had no idea where it was leading but I resisted the temptation to break the silence. I decided to let Giray stew. Regardless, from what he had already confessed there was enough evidence to ban him from Iraq. Sources among the Turkish employees working on the base had given us the rough outlines of his past activities. Giray had filled in the gaps nicely.

Slowly, Giray lifted his head to look at me before looking away. He was tired, dirty, and mentally worn. "Would you rob a man of his last bit of dignity?" I looked at him without blinking. "There was one American soldier from the base. We were friends. We drank, we had fun. He claimed I forced him to have sex. There was a lot of trouble but eventually the charges were dropped. I am not proud of it but it happened."

Relieved that Giray came up with one more item, I was surprised it was such a blockbuster. Forcible sodomy on an American NCO—that was serious stuff. I told Giray I would do my best to help him in his current situation but of course he was already cooked. Lt. Col Tipton, the Base Commander, and Major White were surprised by the total package of info against him. Without hesitation they banned him from the FOB with a note not to allow him access to any bases in Iraq. Giray was on the next convoy to the border with Turkey. Not even his high level friends at HQ could continue to rescue him this time, or so we thought.

Within a few weeks we received word from other Turks that Giray was back and had opened a shop across town on Camp Courage. We contacted the Force Protection there and confirmed that the local command had authorized his return. We could not believe it—Giray had beat us in the end.

12 RAMPANT FAKE IDENTIFICATION

After the fall of Saddam, Iraqi Identification Cards became so unreliable they were next to worthless. Four major forms of identification existed in Iraq: the Gencia, a kind of foldout birth certificate, the Hawiya (Iraqi National ID Card), a passport, and driver's license. Unlike America where the driver's license is king, few Iraqis own them so the document is not common and easily falsified. The most common form of ID is the Hawiya. By law, every Iraqi citizen must maintain one. As I will explain further, these documents were frequently forged. In addition, U.S. military personnel mistakenly called the Hawiya a Gencia. Even official U.S. documents perpetuated this error. So many people called it by the wrong name that you almost had to go along with it. It was an argument difficult to win because most people had accepted the error as fact.

Iraqi officials tried to tighten the security for the Hawiya but it mostly failed. We even knew the locations in the markets where many of the ID were falsified. So, it begs the question, why didn't we try to raid the places and stop the forgery?

First of all, try to imagine the physical context of these locations. Picture a crowded medieval market with narrow alleys like you may have seen in the movies. Thousands of people milling around, most of the merchants know each other and serve as lookout for the others. In the midst of all this sits a non-distinct shop where most citizens know to go for a false ID. The shop may be in the back of a teahouse or craft store. It could operate from almost anywhere. A customer enters from the street and lingers inside where the owners safely observe him for a while. At some point the customer lets them know he needs a false ID. A person will ask a few questions, collect the photos and a small sum of money but the ID is not made there. The material is secretly passed to a courier who will leave by another entrance winding his way through the mazelike back alleys of the bazaar, dropping off the materials to another person who will eventually take it to the forger. Coffee shops provide a great cover for illegal activity because they deliver. Delivery boys come and go constantly and it would be impossible to follow even one without detection. Meanwhile, the customer is normally told to return the next day at a certain time. A few places offer same day service. The operation and location makes it almost impossible to raid or ever reach the forger. If you raid the coffee shop you find nothing. You would not even find one fake ID card because they are produced elsewhere. So the operations are fairly secure from police action.

Even though the problem of fake IDs was serious, it remained the only form of identification available to the U.S. military. Some fakes were better than others but our unit became

156

quite good at detecting them largely due to the excellent work of our security badging NCO, Jason Swope, who developed a keen eye for detecting flaws. Swope was the first line of defense for foreign nationals coming in for screening to obtain access to the base. His sharp eye for detail and outstanding computer skills, brought to the military from his civilian career, helped us foil uncounted attempts to penetrate our base. We routinely detected several phony IDs per day. The perpetrators ranged from common laborers to trusted interpreters. A typical scenario would transpire like the one below.

Early in the day, an Iraqi national Titan terp who had been working for U.S. forces for more than two years down in Baghdad, showed up for routine screening upon his transfer to Mosul. In the access control office, Swope immediately noticed the terp carried a copy of a fake ID. Imagine that, a fake of a fake. Swope terminated his screening and sent him down to me for questioning. Force Protection brought him in and seated him in the interrogation room. A short man, fat in the middle and balding he sat, nervously studying me as I studied him. He was tense but most interviewees were when they reached my interview room. But this one had a kind of arrogant grin, like he was thinking, "I have been through these interviews multiple times before and passed, how dare you make me explain myself again?" We began by reviewing his background, place of birth, tribal association, and family history. All routine topics designed to gather information as well as start the interviewee talking. Not far into the interview we reached the topic of religion.

"You are Sunni Muslim? Do you attend mosque?" I asked.

"I am Muslim in name only, I like to drink and I like to make the fun with women." He grins widely and waits for my reaction but I ignore the remark. We move to discuss his foreign travel. "Yes, I have been to U.S., Tulsa, Oklahoma for training in aircraft mechanics. I have been to Germany, Jordan and Kuwait. Jordan is a good place to have the women," he said.

He is smiling again. I concede a slight smile, but resist the invitation to let him describe his perversions. We talk about his previous employment with Iraqi Airways as a mechanic. Later, he tells me about working as an interpreter for the 101st Airborne and how an RPG wounded him. (You might naturally assume we had the resources to corroborate his U.S. travel but we had no such ability. In fact, we had no way to even verify that he had worked for the 101st Airborne).

"You see, I love Americans," he said.

I am thinking sarcastically, "Oh yes, your story of the RPG, if it is even true, is supposed to convince me to eliminate you as a suspect." Finally, we come to the ID card. "And where did you get this ID?" I asked.

I hold it up in front of me but far enough away so he cannot see it closely. He remains jovial and readily admits the ID is a scanned copy of his "original."

He explains, "I made the copy in case I lose the real one."

Unfortunately for him, I already know the "original" is also a fake. Several discrepancies on the ID match the Tactics, Techniques and Procedures (TTP) for other fake IDs in our possession and seven other people in our system showed the same ID number as him. Three of them are on alert for varying offenses. I ask him where he got it and he starts talking about how he has used it for two years with no problem, avoiding my question. I hate when suspects do that.

Leaning forward and in a more stern voice I repeat, "I asked you WHERE you got it?" This brings him quickly around and back in control.

"A thousand pardons," he apologizes and then names a little copy shop in Baghdad. I ask him when he obtained the "original." He replies, "1991 or '92." Pretty good answer because the issue date on the ID verifies the year 1992. Now comes the more difficult question. I ask him to relate the process of where he went to get it. He looks off to the side and stumbles a little, "I got it in Baghdad."

"Great, but where in Baghdad?" I ask impatiently.

"At the civil affairs office," he replied.

"Where is the office located?"

"I don't remember. It has been a long time." Not a good sign that he is being truthful.

"What does the office look like?"

"Like any other building," he is stuttering, grasping for an answer.

"How many stories is the building?" I ask.

"One," he replies after a slight pause.

"Oh really, Baghdad, a city of several million people has a one story civil affairs office?" He starts to panic at my persistent questioning. "When you enter this building do you turn to the left or right?" He knows I don't believe him but he continues with the tale.

"When you enter you turn right and give your information to a policeman who goes into another room and comes back with the ID."

"Really? The same day?"

He begins to think maybe I detect that was the wrong answer. "No, no, the next day," he stumbles.

"What time?" I continue.

"Aaah, in the afternoon, 2:00 pm," he is anxious.

I am shaking my head no, which adds to his nervousness. "You didn't get this ID at the civil affairs office and you don't know anything about the civil affairs office."

"Yes, I did," he says half defiantly but almost childishly.

"No you didn't." I am looking him straight in the eye and he is quivering. "Look, I know this card is fake, I have a drawer full of ones just like it. I am only interested in where you got it."

He is thinking now. After a long pause he decides to stick to his story. "No, I got it at the civil affairs office." Our eyes are

160

locked and I slowly wag my head from side to side. After a short silence he tries again, "It is very difficult to get a fake ID. Before Saddam fell it was easy but after Saddam fell it was difficult."

"But you got this card in 1992 before Saddam fell," I said.

"That's what I said, before Saddam fell it was difficult and after Saddam fell it was easy," he backtracked.

"No, that's not what you said before."

"No, I meant to say that during the fall of Saddam it was easy but before and afterwards it was difficult." He is quickly tangling in his extemporaneous lies. Sitting back in his chair he shrugs his shoulders, smiles and says laughing, "You can believe me or not, it is the truth."

"Well, I don't believe you and it is not the truth."

He shouts, "I swear by Allah that I got it at the civil affairs office."

Now, I know he is weakening. He has resorted to bringing Allah into the discussion. I try another approach as I slowly walk around his chair. "Look, you have worked around Americans for several years so you know something about our culture." He nods in agreement. I slow the pace of the interview. "Americans are forgiving people, generous people. We can forgive almost anything, but not lying. I know this card is a fake; all I want to learn from you is where you got it. Maybe you bought it in a market, maybe a friend bought it for you?" I try to give him a comfortable way out of this.

THE UNSEEN WAR IN IRAQ

"No," he says curtly.

I commence with the hand demonstration. Holding up my two hands palms facing each other about three feet apart, I begin. Wiggling my right hand I say, "This is the truth," then I wiggle my left, "and this is where you are." I move my left hand closer to the other about a foot. "You started there and now you are here. I want to get to here." I move my hand just a few inches from the right one.

He is looking at the hands and smiling. He leans forward and says, "Yes, I want to get there," pointing at my two hands nearly together.

"Good, that's all I want is the truth. With truth all is made right, with lies…" I pause and cock my head, "we have problems."

"But I will lose my job." His crinkled face betrays his deepest fear.

"Not necessarily, everyone makes mistakes, small mistakes can be fixed. But lies compound little mistakes into big ones." He hunches back in his chair, tired, silence overcomes him as he looks directly at me, searching for a clue as to whether he should finally tell the truth to this American.

After about 15 seconds he mumbles, "THOURA."

"Thoura, what is that?"

"It is a place in Baghdad, Thoura Meridi. I won't lose my job?" his expression is worried.

"Just tell the truth and let's resolve this mess."

"I bought it in Thoura Meridi. It is a place where you go."

"So you bought it in Meridi?"

"Yes."

"Why did you need a fake ID?" I asked.

He smiled again and pointed at me with one finger, "That's a good question. I only wanted to change the year of my birth. I was too old. I was not born in 1960 as my ID says, I was born in 1948."

Helping him relax I laugh, "I wondered about that because you don't look younger than me." He laughed again, starting to lose the nervousness. A little truth will do that.

"It is hard for an old man to find good work. I thought in the confusion during the fall of Saddam, I could change my age, make myself a little younger. Maybe it will even help with the women." He let's out a loud laugh. "I only changed the birth year. All the other information is correct. I have used this ID for two years and no one has questioned it."

I hate that excuse. Weak logic sets my temper rising.

"So because you have acted illegally for two years that makes you innocent?" my voice booming.

His head drops to his chest. "No, I know it was wrong."

"What about at the gate to the base, why didn't they detect it?"

"No, at the gate of FOB Caldwell, an Iraqi interpreter checks the IDs. We understand each other. He tells the soldier it's okay and I pass through."

"Okay," I said, "let's go over the process again. How did you get the ID? Describe Meridi."

"It's a small part of downtown. Café's along the sidewalks, very beautiful. Actually it's quite dangerous. Lots of thieves."

"How do you ask for the ID?" I asked.

"If you go there they know why. You just sit having tea or coffee until someone approaches and asks what you need. Then you say ID, or passport, or driver's license."

"How much did it cost?"

"About 2000 Dinars," he replied.

"And how did you explain your particular desire?"

"I gave him my real ID and a few photos. I told him to make a new one listing my birth year as 1960. In two hours he returned with the ID card. I was afraid I would lose my job if I told the truth. I won't lose my job will I? I will bring my real ID."

"Well, here is what I want, your real ID, the other fake ID, your passport, your gencia and your wife's ID."

"I will do it," he nods with eyes closed for emphasis, "I will go immediately."

"You have two days, come back with all that I ask and we will make things right."

"You are a good man," he says as he puts out his hand to shake mine. "May Allah bless you."

Did we reach the truth? Who knows? He may have changed his entire identity, trying to conceal some criminal background, avoid debts, or erase an embarrassing association with the Saddam regime. For now, we will wait for him to return with his true ID. If he does not return he will be blacklisted and lose a high paying job. If he produces the corroborating ID and all the information matches, we will begin again and make him tell the entire story over in ever increasing detail. We'll dig deeper into his foreign travel, for example, how he got the job with Iraqi Airways without Baath Party membership. If we detect deception, we will pounce on it. Digging for the truth is like performing a root canal. If you stop at the surface decay the painful root is still rotting. You have to drill deep to the absolute bottom to be sure the decay is eliminated. Unfortunately, in Iraq we are capping far too many teeth after only a surface cleaning. So under the guise of partial truth we don't really know for sure who is on our bases and what is their real intention. And what about the Iraqi interpreter at FOB Caldwell, the one that determines which Iraqis enter the post? Very dangerous indeed. Unfortunately, no one will act on it. "Not my lane," will be the answer. It is another bit of information that will slip through the cracks until something blows up. Then questions will be raised and blame arbitrarily assessed.

165

But the IDs are important because they are the beginning point of unraveling the deception. Fake ID represents hard evidence of deception that can be used to ferret out other discrepancies until an acceptable truth is reached. Most military units possessed little knowledge of the fake IDs or the patience to pursue them. Screeners and CI agents ignored the potentially valuable investigative lead because they became caught up in the monotony of simply screening persons for access. To an experienced investigator, the screening process was a goldmine of information that could help uncover all manner of crooks, thieves and most importantly, insurgents.

The false IDs became so normal we began detecting actual patterns of the forgers. Below are a few samples of IDs picked up after we analyzed workers on base with the same or sequentially numbered cards. After calling each person in for questioning, we discovered they all had gained access to our base or others with the false ID. A few cards belonged to laborers who did not even obtain the ID themselves, but instead either paid another person to obtain it or was provided the card by an employment agent supplying workers to the base.

A thousand stories accompanied the false IDs, some more believable than others. Several young men actually changed their age to be old enough to join the Peshmerga Kurdish fighters. This was not uncommon. I recalled another baby faced 20-year old Kurd who came in with a fake ID. He was illiterate but at 20 had already

166

been Pesh for four years. His father gave him the ID and naturally he trusted his father. He loved Americans and had spotted PKK four or five times on the Iraqi side of the Turkish border.[10] His unit commander vouched for the young man so we did not ban him from the base but insisted he obtain a new ID card before we would grant regular access.

Others claimed they needed a fake ID because base security regulations required personnel to surrender their Iraqi ID upon entering the base. Because they did not want to be without their ID, workers bought an additional one in the market. The reason for the regulation rested on our holding their ID as hostage in order to ensure individuals returned their security badge before leaving the base. It was the easiest way to ensure accountability of the access badges. If an employee lost the badge he could, by regulation, lose his job. Concern that our security badges would fall into the hands of insurgents was paramount. Badges could be easily reproduced and Swope changed colors and designs frequently to thwart reproduction but we also controlled the badges in circulation.

One of the fake ID cards in the sequence belonged to a middle-aged female who claimed to have earned a Ph.D. in Arabic

---

[10] PKK refers to a Kurdish terrorist group in eastern Turkey pressing for a separate Kurdish nation.

art and landed a job working for the U.S. government that eventually allowed her to transfer to America. By the time we detected the false ID, she had left for the U.S. and no one wanted to pursue the investigation to verify her bona fides or intentions. After all, we were fighting a war and could not be concerned about a potential immigration violation—at least that was the mindset.

Still other Iraqis could not satisfactorily explain the reasons for possessing a false ID and absent any other evidence against them, they were simply barred from access to the base. Unfortunately, if they changed their name and purchased a new ID in the market, they would likely gain access to another base where the false ID might allow them to slip through the screening process undetected if a lazy or ill-trained screener failed to check carefully or BATS failed to match fingerprints or other biometric data.

Below are a couple of fake Hawiyas. From the samples you can see what an Iraqi ID basically looks like. The forged parts are undetectable to the untrained eye. The faces of the individuals have been blocked out to protect their physical identity. Names alone would not likely be enough to identify them for certain as the names are fake.

13 THE RASPUTIN OF
INTERPRETERS

Unfortunately, identifying a false ID was not always enough to keep a suspicious person from accessing the base. Sometimes economic reasons or emotional ties would cloud the thinking of those involved in the hiring of foreign nationals. One such incident involved a person I called the Rasputin of interpreters because this man just would not seem to die, metaphorically that is. His scenario transpired basically as recorded below.

Mahmood had finally returned and this time we got him— at least that's what we thought. Mahmood was an interesting character. College educated and fluent in English, the handsome Arab was what some would call, a dream interpreter. Tall and friendly with a wide, bright, if not sleazy smile, he emanated a certain charm that attracted Americans. Speaking fluent Farsi in addition to Arabic and English, he denied ever traveling to Iran, claiming a degree in Farsi from Baghdad University. He also claimed a law degree from Mosul University. Unfortunately, despite my consistent objections, we had no mandate to confirm these small but critical facts despite the ease with which we could have done so if not for all applicants, at least for those under suspicion.[11] Mahmood's finer qualities obscured his several failings. Namely, he was a slippery character who had trouble telling the truth, and although Mahmood had passed an initial screening some months before, we were determined to keep a close eye on him. He had arrived on our base several months back with an ID cut off at the bottom, almost a full third missing. The bottom third of the Iraqi national ID contains important data such as the date of issue, the signature of the issuer and the official stamp of the government office that issued it. Some CI agents might have rejected Mahmood instantly without an interview because of his damaged ID card but we felt it useful to document his background and story as many times as possible. In other words, we wanted to document his story before sending him away. Following the interview, we refused to grant him access until he produced complete identification, a simple enough task for an honest man. Instead, Mahmood chose to

---

[11] Vetting simple facts is quite important. Using just one example of Mahmud Abouhalima, the getaway car driver in the 1993 World Trade Center Bombing, Mahmud had remained in the US on an expired tourist visa. His driver's license had been suspended multiple times and had been found guilty of tampering with the seals in his taxicab meter. He applied for amnesty, falsely claiming he was an agricultural worker. Had even the most rudimentary background check been completed, he would have been caught and the entire bombing might have unraveled. In the very least, he would have been deported, thereby disrupting the operation.

disappear, or so we thought. In other words he never returned to our base with the proper identification. Now, months later, he appeared before us again, with more boldness and sure of himself. We soon learned that indeed, Mahmood had not disappeared but had merely moved to another location where his actions did not attract such close scrutiny. He was immediately hired there, inexplicably passing his security screening with the mangled and incomplete ID card we had rejected. While at the new location he skillfully strengthened his reputation among those he served, before seeking a transfer back to Mosul. I was sure he relied on the hope that those of us who knew him had rotated back to America, but unfortunately for him we had not. He seemed quite surprised to see me, at first betraying his concern through a nervous squint in his eyes, then that sleazy smile appeared again as if to mask his fear.

He reached out his hand, damp and slippery, to shake mine, "Hello again my friend," he said, widening his smile as he spoke.

"Well, we have a lot of catching up to do, don't we Mahmood?" I added.

He continued to grin while nodding his head, moving toward the chair hunched over as if sneaking up on it.

Mahmood prepared for his questioning with a kind of cocky assurance. I detected a sense of invulnerability despite the slight nervousness he could not completely conceal. After all, he had been through this type of interview several times now, and was quick to remind me that as a lawyer he knew how to answer questions. He

172

left nothing to chance, even preparing a new ID card. This time however, we had background knowledge to work with, information to compare from his last interview and the comparison proved his undoing.

Not long into the interview Mahmood's story started to unravel under close scrutiny. Previously admitting to Baath Party membership he now erred in the level of his participation. During this interview, he altered the details of his military service including the positions held and ranks achieved. He lied concerning prior illegal activity and drastically changed a previous story about terrorists threatening him and shooting his brother. In a previous interview he claimed insurgents shot his brother in the right leg. In this interview, Mahmood reported that his brother had been shot in the left arm. Other inconsistencies emerged forcing Mahmood to stumble in his explanation and causing anxiety to appear on his face even as the beads of sweat formed on his forehead. His feeling of invulnerability had turned into a sense of danger for the safety of whatever secret he tried desperately to conceal. His new ID card too, had troubling inconsistencies relating to his previous one, leading me to believe that one of them was a fake. Mahmood failed the re-screening miserably. I recommended an in-depth investigation be opened on him but for a number of reasons he was ultimately denied access and removed from the base, which should have meant an automatic firing from Titan, his employer. Based on information we developed, it would not be unreasonable to suspect he might be working for the insurgency or even for Iranian intelligence. At any rate, his multiple stories should have been investigated and corroborated independently. But the expedient of barring him from access was the route chosen by local command, which was its only practical option. Force Protection could not open investigations and MI had no resources for such action at that time. Even if we could have convinced them to investigate it would have taken time requiring us to hold Mahmood until completed. No provision existed for this either. It would have been much easier to allow us to verify the easy items such as education records but we were not authorized. So Mahmood was simply denied access to military installations in Iraq.

Ironically, our action galled the C-2 (the military intelligence officer on the HQ staff) because upon hearing the outcome of our interview, CI screeners from Camp Courage complained that we should not re-screen people they had already passed, and the head of that unit was a personal friend of the C-2. Instead of showing interest that we may have exposed a potential insurgent or possible Iranian intelligence agent, as well as exposing vulnerabilities in our system, the unit and the C-2, interpreted our action as a slight to their professionalism, oddly taking the side of Mahmood, arguing that a person screened at one location should be cleared for access to any installation in Iraq. It presented well in theory but we had learned the hard way that each unit does not screen with the same rigor, a problem that haunted us throughout the year. Our Base Commander and Force Protection OIC would not risk relying on the professionalism of screeners from another location they did not know. They correctly insisted that to obtain access to FOB Marez, all Iraqis had to pass our screening process forcing Mahmood to stand before us once again that day.

We expected some fallout from this because Mahmood was popular with his unit as well as highly capable. However, we did not anticipate the degree of resistance we would encounter. First of all, Titan could not accept that Mahmood had failed the security screening. Titan, the company contracted to provide translators to the U.S. Army, demanded to know why he had failed. Mahmood was loved by the military unit to which he was assigned and they did not want to lose him. Simultaneously, Titan was under pressure to fill vacant interpreter slots or possibly lose the entire high dollar value contract. Not only did the company lose money when a slot remained unfilled but mounting vacancies placed the company's contract at risk. Company officials pulled out all the stops to save him, first, complaining to the C-2 that we were unfair, then that our screening was unduly rigorous and unnecessary. At the same time they summoned their own Force Protection representative from Baghdad to persuade me to change the "failed" screening to a "pass." I met the representative (Jack) and he offered most of the same arguments I had heard from the C-2 so I knew they had also talked.

Jack began by trying to impress me with his background. "My boss sent me up here to see what the heck is going on. I am prior Special Forces with eight years experience," he began with his chest puffed a little.

"Oh really," I said, "and how many of those years did you work in CI?"

"None," he said, slightly deflated.

"Okay, just so you know, I worked in CI most of my military career as an officer, head of country level CI and as a commander." He quickly shifted to a different topic.

"Well, we want to know why Mahmood did not pass his CI screening. He has been a great employee. This isn't fair. We have to get these people hired."

First of all, there is a conflict of interest in telling anyone outside the CI chain, especially a civilian contractor, the reasons for a person failing the security interview. Outsiders had no need to know and in fact were prohibited from this knowledge by military regulation. In the past, sponsors in general, and Titan in particular, had told candidates why they had failed revealing vital TTP. If any candidates applied under the direction of the insurgency (which they sometimes did), the insurgency could gain valuable insight into what criteria we used to screen them and how future candidates might answer to help defeat our questioning.

"What's the matter, don't you trust us?" he asked.

The short answer would be "No." I really don't trust anyone with information they have no need to know and a monetary interest for not protecting it. As Jack had already stated, "We have to get these people hired." Our unit had plenty of experience with situations where we had told trusted members from military and civilian sponsors why their particular candidate did not pass and they went right outside and immediately coached the person on what to say in order to convince us the candidate was truthful and it had all been a big mistake. My answer to Jack was "No, you cannot know why he failed the screening, period."

Jack tried a different tack. Is this person a security risk? If so, how? And if so we need to know in what way? Once again, Jack was way off base.

I informed him that, "By definition, failing the screening interview qualifies the person as a security risk, and disqualifies him for access to the base." Sponsors need know nothing more and that fact alone should be the basis for termination.

Then he tried the argument that raised my hackles as much as any for its illogic. "But he has worked for us for two years. Surely, if he were a risk we would have discovered it by now." I explained that longevity does not lessen the security risk of any individual. In one sense, interpreters who have served with Coalition Forces the longest present a greater risk in that they could have been turned by insurgents at any time during their long tenure, and because they have built trust with their sponsors they often escaped the kind of close scrutiny and suspicion that a new member might encounter. In this sense, the longer they worked for us the safer it was for an AIF (Anti-Iraqi Force) infiltrator to operate. Periodic re-screening can sometimes help uncover a person who had gone undetected for a long period.

Next, Jack dropped the bombshell. Attempting to turn one CI element against another he said, "But he has passed previous screenings. Are you saying that your colleagues at other locations are unprofessional?" Titan thought this argument would be successful for two reasons. First, no one likes to impugn a colleague. We all prefer to assume that everyone is professional. Secondly, if Titan could cause us to admit that our system had problems, it might successfully blame its unfilled slots on our screening process, a tactic which their representatives had tried in the past. As for the first reason, true, colleagues do not challenge the professionalism of each other lightly. However, we had mounting evidence that the process at one location was particularly sloppy, and the safety of our troops trumped the feelings of colleagues. So, as politely as possible we were admitting that at least a few locations employed bad apples or at least those who were not as rigorous in applying prescribed methods.

But there is another operational aspect that remained just as important. Even when it works properly, the system generally requires time to yield results. In other words, it often takes time for applicants to slip up. It may take until the second or third interview for inconsistencies in his story to surface. This might seem strange to outsiders but perfectly expected by CI Agents. Even after explaining this, Jack remained undeterred. In fact, he convinced me that he was not interested in logic, he had been sent on a mission to get Mahmood rehired and had no intention of allowing facts to dissuade him.

Feeling the pain of having his arguments shot down one by one, Jack played what he thought was his ace in the hole. Reaching for a short stack of papers that he had been playing with off and on during our conversation but had temporarily laid aside, he now raised it high and then slammed it down spreading the sheets out in front of me like a Las Vegas card dealer. "But I have all these letters of recommendations from units," grinning broadly as he spoke, "are they all wrong and you the only one that is right?" He quickly gathered them together and handed the stack to me to read.

Again, this argument was so shallow and demonstrated such ignorance coupled with disregard for the safety of the troops that I started to become angry. Letters for interpreters from units are almost perfunctory and have little relevance to the counter-intelligence assessment. The intention of an insurgent or espionage agent is to endear himself to the sponsor and develop a strong cover to place himself beyond suspicion. Obviously, it helps to ask the unit to provide a letter extolling the virtue and good work of the interpreter. Most units are only too glad to oblige. Military units have little to reward terps with since they cannot give them cash.

What they can offer is a letter of thanks for their service. Such letters carry sentimental value to honest terps. Titan allowed the letters to be placed in individual personnel files to support the company's claim of providing top-notch employees to the government or to bolster fights against termination such as this one. I took the entire stack out of his hand and threw it straight into the garbage can in one clean shot.

"Those letters are meaningless," I barked. "Units have little knowledge of CI and are often blinded to the hidden agenda of those working for the other side. Do not confuse a unit's emotional preference for a terp as validation that he is clean." Jack appeared shell shocked, sitting bewildered for a moment then returning to a new twist on an old argument.[12]

"But how can one base's screenings be more stringent than another?" he persisted.

In human intelligence, the human factor is definitely a variable. While standards are in place, the experience and

---

[12] Worldnetdaily.com reported that in 2007, a Titan translator plead guilty in a U.S. district court in Brooklyn, N.Y., to possessing classified information and passing it to Iraqi insurgents. The report noted, "The irony is that his military superiors reportedly gave him high marks for his work with an intelligence unit in Iraq." See Gordon, Jerry. "An Intelligence Disaster in Iraq." Worldnetdaily.com. 1 March 2007. 23 July 2008 <http://worldnetdaily.com/index.php?fa=PAGE.view&pageId=40409>.

thoroughness of the screener or interviewer will always play some part in the quality of the process. Throughout Iraq, we suffered a hodgepodge of experience levels, some agents with as little as one or two years of experience. Others claimed military intelligence backgrounds but not in interrogations or operations. A few had served in support of administrative functions while others may have conducted vulnerability surveys or similar general duties, with very limited exposure to actual investigations or interrogating suspects. Screenings conducted by those persons could not be expected to achieve the same thoroughness as seasoned agents.

In addition, a Base Commander can always be more restrictive if it contributes to the safety and security of the installation. Our commander wisely took the more restrictive approach, which was reasonable considering the DFAC bombing had occurred only months earlier on our very base. The truth be told, variations in screenings should be expected but that's not what these people wanted to hear. Regardless, Mahmood's denial of access stood and Jack and his boss clearly did not like it. Contractor company officials complained vigorously to the C-2.

Only days later I learned the most disturbing news. Company officials removed Mahmood from access to U.S. Forces but pulled a dirty trick; they transferred him to British Forces. In my opinion, this was the lowest of moves and clearly disregarded the safety of troops. I was told the Brits hired terps from the same company as the U.S. but under a different contract. A friend in the system also told me that we did not share the derogatory information from our database routinely, so the Brits had no way of knowing Mahmood had been denied access for security reasons by U.S. Forces. That is, they would have known had the company been honest with them. I can't imagine the Brits hiring such a person without inquiring further had they been told why he was denied access by us. In the chance that Mahmood was working for AIF, British forces would have been in danger. I was worried for the Brits but had no way to directly contact them and such action would have been way outside my lane. I complained up through the C-2 level but it fell on deaf ears, even though the C-2 had access to our full classified report. What concerned me even more was the nagging question of whether the company had pulled the same trick on U.S. Forces, transferring a suspicious person from the Brits to us without providing the full history of his background. I was livid that a company could disregard all of our safety for the sake of money. Unfortunately, nothing would come of it.

14 THE ONE THAT GOT AWAY

Battling the bureaucracy of the government can be frustrating, but if one persists long enough he can usually overcome it. Below is a case where I would have to chalk one up to the other side with an assist from our own bureaucracy. Yes, on this day, the failings of our own system helped defeat our best efforts. Late in the afternoon, elements from one of our Striker Brigades brought in an individual called Bassam. Thin and soft spoken, he seemed meek and gentle. As one of the interpreters for the unit, Bassam had been making his coworkers uncomfortable by acting a tad too curious about tactical operations. Even the other Iraqi terps were said to be suspicious. Seasoned terps trust no one, as they know that any Iraqi that betrays them could cost their lives or the lives of their loved ones. In general, terps do not reveal much personal information to their colleagues as an extra precaution. At the same time, it is in their best interest to report someone they suspect may be working for AIF, as it might save their own life as well as the soldiers they work with. Insurgents delight in infiltrating U.S. military units, if for no other reason than to identify Iraqis working for U.S. Forces that can be intimidated, threatened or turned to work for them while keeping their jobs within the U.S. system.

Representatives of a unit I will call A-1, asked if our office could re-screen Bassam in the off chance we could confirm which side he was truly on. Two sergeants from A-1 confided they really did not want Bassam back in the unit until they received some type of answer or assurance from us as to whose side he was really on. It was an awesome responsibility in one sense. These troops were depending on us to determine the trustworthiness of a badly needed terp in a short amount of time. If we judged an innocent terp as untrustworthy and caused his removal, the unit may well have to function without benefit of translation, which could ultimately endanger them while on patrol. On the other hand, if we failed to detect the dishonest terp who could be working for the AIF, then we would obviously be endangering our troops in another way. We always erred on the side of caution but in most cases the terps skillfully endeared themselves to the unit, playing on the kindness and trust of the soldiers and bonding in a way that blinded the troops to infiltrators who had gained that trust falsely. In some cases, even when we uncovered a terp believed to be working with AIF, high-ranking members of the unit would defend him, trying to retain the terp on duty. But A-1 was different. They were sharp enough to recognize the danger and seek help. Our office built a solid reputation of ferreting out potential AIF in our midst and units routinely brought suspect members to us for a checkup. My goal was to remain as objective as possible but always erring on the side of protecting the safety of our troops. I tried just as hard to exonerate a suspect as to expose one because I knew the units needed interpreters badly to function safely. At the same time, we obviously needed trustworthy terps and if there was any doubt, they were removed. Our Force Protection OIC, Major White, earned a reputation for throwing people off the FOB for the slightest infraction. "OTF" (off the FOB) became his mantra. This strong stance was critical in helping us clean up the base at Mosul.

As guards escorted Bassam into the interrogation room he looked around seemingly at everything almost without thinking. Beads of sweat already formed above his eyebrows. He was nervous without question, but we expected some anxiety. Anyone sent for questioning worried about the outcome. Justified or not, rumors among the Iraqis spread that one slip could land a person in the detention facility or even worse, Abu Ghraib prison. It was our job to discern whether the interviewee's nervousness was normal or produced by guilt, hiding something he feared we might uncover. Every interrogator makes these subjective judgments, partly in an initial observation and partly in an overall assessment. We obtained Bassam's basic biometrics to check him out in our database by name, date of birth, Iraqi ID number and other background information we elicited from him. Then, Bassam stepped up to the fingerprint device. As I touched his hand, a sweaty palm and fingers reminded me to put on the surgical gloves before continuing. The computer scanned all ten fingers, theoretically for comparison with all the other locally employed persons (LEPs) and detainees in

Iraq, a database of several hundred thousand persons. Next we photographed him, careful to obtain a picture with enough facial elements to allow another comparison. Finally, we electronically scanned his eyes which acted like a fingerprint, able to be checked in the same database. Nothing showed up on Bassam. As I mentioned previously, unfortunately for us, even with all the so-called high technology, rarely did the database produce usable hits, partly because data input into BATS varied by location. Each location with the capability to enter data into the system treated the process slightly differently. Some units took the time to enter the data properly, others didn't; some entered partial data. If a soldier snapped a photo that wasn't quite detailed enough for identification, he should take the time to shoot it again, but if for whatever reason he decided not to, then the picture would remain in the system but not usable for computer comparison. The same with fingerprints and eye scans. The computer would accept fingerprints of reduced quality but would not be able to compare them well. A few soldiers applied their G.I. humor by including pictures of their butts or other funny scenes in the database. An analysis of the system once by a visiting team of auditors produced hundreds of these kinds of entries but that report was squelched; I was told not to mention it. Even when soldiers faithfully entered data, they might enter inaccurate info unknowingly. With the abundance of false ID cards in Iraq, one never knew how accurate the data in the system really was. Untrained soldiers could not spot fake IDs easily. As discussed above, our unit pioneered effective countermeasures for false IDs and seized hundreds of them during our tour. But even if all the previous steps were correctly followed, the database itself had major deficiencies. In short, it did not work properly. Basically, the government had been sold a bill of goods for hundreds of millions of dollars that had limited value. Multiple times we checked known fingerprints and eye scans without generating hits in the database. No one wanted to admit it but the database had been corrupted several times along the way. On one occasion, the main computer crashed deleting thousands of files and partially destroying thousands of others. It frustrated us to see files we had painstakingly entered turn up with most of the data missing.

Bassam's case was even more disturbing. Soldiers from the unit told us that Bassam had worked over at Camp Courage twice in the last two years. He quit there and showed up at FOB Marez, where Titan rehired him as a terp raising his salary from $350 to $1,050 per month. However, nothing of his employment showed up in the system. The HUMINT Support Team at Courage also screened him several months prior, but again, nothing in the system.

CI is neither voodoo nor magic, although it can be a strange mixture of art and science, objective and subjective judgment. A thorough initial screening with interview takes about two hours. Even the best interrogator is unlikely to expose the most amateur AIF in the first interview. If Bassam's information from the previous interviews had been in the database we could have used it to test his truthfulness. If he had lied in the past or was lying now, we might be able to catch him since it is increasingly difficult to remember lies told months before under pressure of interrogation. Since Bassam did not turn up in the database we had nothing to compare. We conducted the interview blind and allowed Bassam to establish a "story." He appeared deceptive in certain areas but nothing we could pinpoint. Later, another interpreter on our team recognized Bassam and told me that on a previous assignment with THT 292, Bassam had been interviewed twice under suspicion of involvement in providing AIF intelligence that may have led to the kidnapping of terps back in 2004. Unfortunately, not only had Bassam been released but had been returned to duty. Our interpreter, who was a U.S. citizen not a local national, worked for the THT at the time and had translated during the interviews. This proved a tremendous break for us. Now, we might have a chance to determine once and for all if Bassam was helping AIF from the inside. I tried to contact the THT that had interviewed him before but learned it had rotated back to the States long ago leaving no records behind. Units routinely took their files and equipment with them when they rotated back to America.

We faced another more pressing problem. Bassam was in our hands and we had very limited time to deal with him. All we had at this point were a few suspicions and possible leads but the clock worked against us confirming the information in time. The end of the day approached quickly and we needed to decide what to do with Bassam. Technically, he remained in custody of Force Protection but they had no capability to hold prisoners overnight. Force Protection had no jail to hold him. They could assign a person to guard him all night, but they were already undermanned for their regular duties and could not spare anyone. We needed to buy time to develop more information on this case and our best option was to send him to the BIF (Battalion Interrogation Facility) overnight and pick him up in the morning. The BIF is a battalion level detention facility with the capability to feed, house and guard prisoners in a secure area. There was also a DIF over on MAF, an even more secure facility designed for long term detention, but we needed solid evidence before they would accept prisoners there. The reality remained that we could either hold him in the BIF or release him. Constantly coordinating with Major White, we agreed letting him go was unthinkable because Bassam could very likely pose an intelligence threat. Force Protection had the authority to hold suspects 72 hours to allow time to gather pertinent information. We had used the BIF in the past to hold suspects overnight, but the BIF had recently changed hands with the arrival of A-1. The old unit had rotated out and the new guys were adding their own touch to the facility.

While all this was developing, I had been trying to turn Bassam over to a THT for further interrogation. At the time there was only one THT assigned to the base and it was TDY (temporary duty) to another location. Two other THTs were DS, army terminology meaning direct support to a specific unit. Both DS THTs were not available all day as they were out on patrol with their units. That was their function, to support the units directly and they were not responsible for CI inside the wire. Since Bassam worked for A-1, I thought it best to at least coordinate with A-1's THT. With the duty day quickly coming to an end, I had to arrange for Bassam's overnight stay which could take hours to coordinate. Around 6:00 pm I finally tracked down A-1s THT. I explained the situation to Sgt Shields, a young female interrogator who was bright and energetic but lacked experience and confidence. She promised to take Bassam to the BIF and work with us on interrogating him the following day. I hung up relieved and began preparing a list of questions and leads to follow-up on the next morning. Within ten minutes, Sgt Shields called me back frantic and confused. She apologized and explained that her S-2 (intelligence staff), a young Captain, told her not to take Bassam into custody and not to place him in the BIF. The Captain said that higher headquarters (Brigade) had notified him it was against the law (U.S. Code Title 10), to place Bassam in the BIF or even for the THT to interview him. Brigade had rendered the judgment that even though Bassam was a local national, because he worked under contract with the U.S. as a terp he must be treated as a U.S. person with all the rights and privileges thereof. Someone at the Brigade level had told the Captain in the Battalion S-2 this was now an espionage investigation of a U.S. person and THT had no authority to conduct those. An officer at Brigade further warned the S-2 to back off this case because TFF would take over and if there were any questions to call Major Smith the C2X at TFF Headquarters.

I sat stunned in my chair. This reasoning represented incompetence at its worst and I could not believe what I had heard. "No use arguing with Sgt Shields," I thought. She labored at the bottom of the totem pole and could do nothing. I told her I would call right back and quickly hung up to call Major Smith. He knew nothing about what the Brigade staff officer had told the Battalion S-2 but he promised to check into it. Quickly switching gears, I contacted "C" Company 1Sgt Jones. "C" Company originally brought Bassam to me. Angry at the run around we experienced, 1Sgt Jones promised he would place Bassam into the BIF. Within a short time he sent over a few soldiers to take Bassam into custody and escort him to the jail. I coordinated with Major White and the Base Commander, who approved my actions and the three of us shook our heads in disbelief that we were encountering this much difficulty holding on to a suspicious person who could be endangering our troops by providing operational info to AIF.

The next morning, I visited 1Sgt Jones early and discovered that Bassam never made it into the BIF. The 1Sgt was furious that his S-2 could not be persuaded to stand up for what was right. The S-2 told 1Sgt Jones to either kick him off the base or guard Bassam himself. 1Sgt Jones held Bassam under guard in the Company area overnight. I immediately went about interviewing Bassam's roommates gaining troubling firsthand information that could be used against him in the future. It quickly became clear that Bassam had a little too much interest in operational matters such as times of patrols, their routes, how many soldiers lived on the base, and the specific locations of sister units, among other sensitive items that he had no need to know. In addition, Bassam had mentioned to his coworkers that in 2004 terrorists slid a note under his door threatening to kill him which caused him to quit working for a time. This differed from the "story" he related to me in the initial interview. Lying to me only weakened his case and raised suspicions even further. 1Sgt Jones and I decided to visit the S-2 in the TOC (Tactical Operations Center) to discuss the gravity of the information we continued to develop confirming the importance of buying additional time to investigate, but the S-2 would hear none of it. He insisted that Brigade had warned him it was against the law to hold Bassam and that TFF would send down a special team to take over the investigation. Even after I informed him I had talked to the C2X personally and no team was coming, the young Captain would not budge, afraid of bucking Brigade.

We were left with a curious dilemma. A-1's THT was forbidden to interrogate Bassam. No other THT was available to interrogate him. Under Army rules, I was prohibited from pursuing this much further and should have turned over the matter to a THT, but we had no one willing to take him. Bassam should have been thoroughly interrogated to determine if he acted under the direction of AIF. It would have been best to continue developing information that might have been actionable later and Major White agreed I should continue to do so. The Base Commander and Major White traveled to TFF that day and discussed the issue. While I waited for Lt Col Tipton and Major White to return to lend some rank to the resolution of this issue, Bassam remained under guard in the Company area all day. But given their mission requirements for patrolling the city, "C" Company lacked the manpower to guard Bassam 24 hours a day. Without additional manning and no support from their higher headquarters on pursuing this matter, A-1 released Bassam out the front gate at 1600 hours. We were all in a rage including their 1Sgt. We tagged Bassam in BATS but he will likely show up again at another base trying to gain access under another identity. We missed an excellent opportunity to exploit a potential intelligence threat to the base. Major White and I raised the problem to higher headquarters immediately. A day later they realized their mistake. I wrote a policy paper suggesting how to prevent this from happening again, but like so many problems, it was entrusted to the corporate memory of those in positions of authority at the time to remember it and those people rotated regularly.

We lost a highly suspicious person that day due to bureaucratic fog and a few inexperienced bureaucrats. Older hands like the 1SGT were livid. Like us, he clearly saw the ramifications of this situation. But bureaucracy and inexperience could defeat us in other ways. The case of Abdul Sulayman comes to mind.

15 ABDUL SULAYMAN

Abdul Sulayman was an interesting character; round faced and jovial he looked like an Iraqi Santa Clause. Always smiling, he was an amiable person, well-liked by almost everyone who knew him. He had worked for General Saladin, a retired Iraqi General Officer, who owned a large Iraqi restaurant on base, itself an item of contention. Saladin had the exclusive right to run this restaurant on base without paying rent, claiming a ranking U.S. Army General gave him that right several years before when Saladin agreed to provide local food to U.S. soldiers at great risk to himself during the initial occupation of Mosul. The problem with Saladin's story was that no general had the authority to grant such permission, and it should not have been honored several years later, but no one wanted to cross Saladin because of his friendship with the high ranking U.S. General, long since gone from Iraq but still in theater. My investigator instinct told me Saladin was at the least crooked and at the worst, tied to the insurgency. We interviewed him several times and he ended up moving to the UAE for a while to avoid scrutiny.

Saladin groomed and protected his friend Abdul who appeared to have branched out on his own, making friends among the U.S. officers and gaining contracts to supply the base with certain items. However, in my office, we heard rumors of his criminal involvement in a long list of issues on base but were never able to gather enough evidence and the Criminal Investigations Division (CID) was not interested in these matters. At the time they were almost exclusively focused on prisoner abuse cases.

This time we thought that we had him cold. We summoned him for re-interview because we strongly suspected he used false identification to enter the installation. His ID number had shown up in a sequence of false ID cards uncovered by the brilliant work of Jason Swope, which was covered previously in the chapter on Fake ID. Abdul had been around the block. Survival skills learned under Saddam's regime worked well with Americans. He took special effort to befriend senior American officers on the base and became trusted by command officials as well as former general officers whose names Abdul was quick to drop whenever he had the chance.

Abdul had moved his family to Amman Jordan because, he said, he felt more secure there. During our interview he disclosed that he had recently traveled to Istanbul on business for about two weeks. He appeared nervous, unaccustomed to being questioned or having to explain his past in detail. He carefully cultivated his relationship with certain command officials to provide protection for occasions just as these, making sure to remind me that he had never had to sit for such questioning in the past and that maybe I should call a few of his high ranking friends to clear up the matter. I tried to put him at ease, massaging his ego by explaining the questions were mostly routine but were needed to round out the information in our file and that as long as he was honest, the interview would proceed smoothly. I assured him he was an important and respected man, well known to key personnel on base. He visibly relaxed some at that thought. I added how impressed I was with his interesting past and hoped he would share more of it with us. We began talking about his former membership in the Baath Party. In a previous interview, he stated he only achieved the Muayyid level (sympathizer). This time Abdul said he rose to Odu—three levels higher. I chose not to mention yet that he had previously given different information. Although not an expert in Baath Party membership, our guidance from Multi National Force Iraq (MNF-I) was that the Baath Party had ten levels, beginning with Sadiq (friend) entry level and ending with UDW Qiyadah (Member of the Leadership level—see chart later in this chapter).

Coalition Provisional Authority (CPA) Order Number 1, issued in 2003 ordered the De-Ba'Athification of Iraqi Society. Ambassador Paul Bremer signed it, ordering full members in senior leadership positions, from level 7-10, removed immediately and banned from public service. He also ordered that the top three layers of management in every government ministry, affiliated corporations and other government institutions including hospitals and universities would be interviewed to determine what level they had reached in the Party. Section 3 stated that, "Any such persons determined to be full members of the Baath Party shall be removed

196

from their employment." This included everyone level 5 or higher.[13] Hatred ran high against former Baath Party members, especially among the Shiite community who accused them of crimes against the Iraqi people. Others argued that, like it or not, former Baathists had the knowledge to run key government agencies and industries. By denying them employment, Iraq continued to suffer. The policy stayed in effect, even after the new Iraqi government was formed, until January 2008 when in the spirit of reconciliation, the Iraqi Parliament enacted legislation allowing all but the highest members of the former party to return to work.[14]

I don't know when or how it changed, but the military pretty much accepted the notion that to gain any position of consequence in Iraq from teacher to government official, to trusted military officer, one had to join the Baath Party. Membership represented a certain loyalty to Saddam. Initially, those who wanted to work with the U.S. government tried to conceal previous ties with the former regime, including Baath Party affiliation. Later, they

---

[13] See CPA /ORD/16 May 2003/01, De-Ba'Athification of Iraqi Society.

[14] Oppel, Jr., Richard A. and Steven Lee Myers. "Iraq Eases Curb on Ex-Officials of Baath Party." New York Times. 13 Jan. 2008. 3 Aug. 2008 <http://www.nytimes.com/2008/01/13/world/middleeast/13iraq.html?ex=1357880400&en=308b9bac9a092481&ei=5088&partner=rssnyt&emc=rss>.

learned that the U.S. deemed it impractical to disqualify those at the lowest levels of membership who had no real loyalty to Saddam but joined the party out of necessity. The U.S. military did draw the line at the Odu or Member level. If a person attained Udw Qiyadat Firqah (Group Leadership Member) or higher, they were automatically excluded from employment with the U.S. military. The rationale was that to advance beyond Odu, one had to be an active trusted party member, completing multiple levels of training and demonstrating devotion to the regime. It didn't take long for Iraqis to identify the Odu threshold. So it became routine for Iraqis to admit party membership at the Muayyid or Nassir levels but were careful not to admit membership above Odu. Abdul was no exception.

Levels of the Iraqi Baath Party

1. Friend   (SADIQ)
2. Sympathizer   (MUAYYID)
3. Supporter   (NASSIR AWWAL)
4. Advanced Supporter   (NASSIR MUTAQADDAM)
5. Member   (ODU)
6. Active Member   (UDW AMIL)
7. Group Leadership Member   (UDW QIYADAT FIRQAH)
8. Section Member   (UDW SHUBAH)
9. Branch Member   (UDW FIARA)
10. Member of the Leadership   (UDW QIYADAH)

We moved the discussion to his prior military experience. Abdul claimed he worked in Iraqi Security in charge of targeting. He tried to skirt the possibility he may have worked in intelligence. Abdul confided that he carried a top-secret security clearance and that as a Colonel in the Iraqi Air Force, he dealt with the intelligence service regularly providing required reports and information. Smiling broadly, Abdul boasted he knew over 100 intelligence officers like General Aziz, but added the caveat that he never learned their full names. In answers to my questions, he explained that some of the former intelligence officers still lived in the Mosul area but most remained in hiding or had been caught by U.S. forces. One in particular, Colonel Kareem Hassan Ali, had been the director of Section Eight of Iraqi intelligence in Baghdad. Abdul explained that the former Iraqi intelligence field consisted of 15 sections, each with a specific function. Personnel in Section Eight monitored the officers who worked in the military field offices around Iraq. Half excited, Abdul added that Colonel Ali became a businessman currently supplying the FOBs with air conditioning units through Colonel Abdul's company. When asked if Colonel Ali was not one of the men that should be in hiding from U.S. Forces, Colonel Abdul replied, "No, Colonel Ali is a good man." I wanted to bring in Colonel Ali for questioning. Surely, the former Section Chief of Iraqi intelligence would be of interest to our intelligence branch. From a CI perspective, the thought of a former known intelligence officer supplying our bases set off alarm bells.

He likely obtained general access to several bases, yet there was no record in BATS that he had ever been screened. Who knew for certain which side he worked for? A trained intelligence agent could easily gather all sorts of information for the insurgency, even working with Colonel Abdul to collect it. With their connections, and the trust built with U.S. Forces, the two could prove to be a gem for the insurgency. I decided not to show too much interest at that time, not wanting to alarm Abdul or raise the slightest suspicion.

I slowly changed the subject to his ID card, which I already knew was fake. Asked where he obtained his ID, Colonel Abdul insisted that he applied for it at the government office in Mosul. However, he stumbled when asked to explain the location of the office and the details of the procedures followed to obtain it. He concocted an elaborate story of how he went to the civil affairs office to apply for the ID. Just to add a little pressure, I mentioned that I was quite familiar with the process and the location. I swear I heard a giant gulp at that point. Abdul failed this part of the questioning miserably and after having been caught in this lie, finally admitted he had two IDs, one fake and one real. But he continued to weave a different lie. He now decided to insist that the fake ID was just an exact copy of his original. I knew this was also untrue because it was in sequence with other fakes we had seized from workers on base, but of course Abdul did not know what I knew. His second lie demonstrated another clear act of deception, which was in itself grounds for expulsion from the base. I softly confronted Abdul's lie by telling him that he had used a different ID during a previous interview. In fact, I did not know if he did so but I made him think I knew that he did.

Now, he slipped his cover and in a show of disgust blurted out, "That was my mistake. The only way you caught me was not using the same ID in both interviews."

Clearly, Abdul had been lying and deceiving U.S. Forces for some time. I was tempted to call for SF to hood him and whisk him away to a safe house for full interrogation but I continued calmly. Abdul eventually explained there were several places to purchase fake IDs behind the Mosul police station. For security reasons, he did not purchase the fake ID himself but sent his driver with money and pictures. The fake passport cost $130 and the fake ID $30.

Fake passports are more of an international problem than a local Iraqi problem. According to Interpol, some 3,000 people a week try to enter a country using stolen, altered or completely fraudulent passports. Interpol Secretary General Ron Noble once put it this way, "Every significant international terrorist attack that has occurred has been linked in some way with fraudulent passports, an authentic passport that has been modified or with a counterfeit passport."[15] Within Iraq, we were concerned more with the fake ID which could help him gain access to our bases.

Abdul claimed he needed a fake ID for when he traveled but he had been using it on base for the last two years. He worried about losing access to the base so I reassured him that such a matter could be worked out for a man of his importance and loyalty. I told him that although the regulations called for him to be banned from all installations for using false ID, we would help him if he would help us. I asked him to return with his true ID and Colonel Ali so that we could have lunch together and I could learn some of the history of his old days under Saddam, explaining that such knowledge would be of great value to U.S. forces. Abdul agreed it could be arranged. Of course, I had no intention of having lunch with either Colonel but would arrange for the military to take them both into custody upon returning.

My assessment to command was that Abdul had multiple strikes against him and posed a potential threat to security:

He had used false ID to gain access to a U.S. installation, (normally enough for automatic expulsion).

------

[15] "The Man from Interpol." Noble, Ron. Reported by Steve Kroft. 60 Minutes. CBS. KDKA, Pittsburgh. 7 Oct. 2007. 21 July 2008 <http://www.cbsnews.com/sections/i_video/main500251.shtml?id=33 40375n>.

He stated that his only mistake was not using the same ID in both interviews. (Clear act of deception, enough by itself for automatic expulsion).

He stated the ID he initially presented was an exact copy of the original. It was not. (Deception—automatic expulsion).

He made multiple attempts to conceal his second ID until tripped up in questioning. (Deception – grounds for automatic expulsion).

He fabricated a detailed story of how he obtained the ID from the civil affairs office. (Deception—automatic expulsion).

His false ID was one in a series of sequential numbers, all false IDs of workers on base. (Deception—automatic expulsion).

He was a skilled liar, well trained in intelligence interviewing. Another reason to suspect he was former Iraqi intelligence not security.

He admitted knowing more than 100 former intelligence officers many of whom were from Mosul. (Justification for in-depth interrogation).

He maintains relations with the former head of Section Eight of Iraqi Intelligence. In fact he used him as a subcontractor for multiple FOBs. (CI threat—possible arrest).

He held a top-secret clearance in the Iraqi Air Force and worked in targeting. (Reason for further interrogation).

He failed to disclose his full background information in a screening interview. (Automatic expulsion).

Possibly concealing his true level in the former Baath Party. (Reason for further investigation and interview.)

Unfortunately, his U.S. military connections quickly began paying off. A number of senior officers who knew and liked him began to voice vigorous resistance that such a kind man could be an intelligence officer or work against U.S. interests. That I had to argue such a case about a man with this shady background was hard for me to believe. Luckily, with help from the C-2 office we were able to fend off his protectors.

Debaathification sometimes created a sticky situation. In 2005, we received news that Mosul airfield would soon be turned over to the Iraqi government and reopened as a civilian airport again. The transfer would occur slowly and in stages but the U.S. was actively searching for Iraqis who could run the operation. Iraqi officials selected to work there must be screened to determine their trustworthiness. Military officials were in contact with one former Iraqi Air Force Lt. Col who used to run the airfield under Saddam. In fact, they quietly provided him a pension keeping him on the payroll until just such an occasion when he could be of use. Unfortunately, our background screening revealed his high Baath Party affiliation and connection with former Iraqi Intelligence. That disqualified him under the rules. Personally, I thought the man sincere and merely doing what he had to do to survive under Saddam. He provided honest and candid answers to us but at that time Command disqualified him for the job due to the regulation.

16 A Suspicious Kurd

In general, the Kurdish people are great friends of America and honest to a fault. I grew fond of them during my tour in Iraq. However, crime and espionage knows no ethnic or racial boundaries. Al Qaeda maintains a deadly Kurdish offshoot known as Ansar al-Islam, responsible for bombings and intelligence gathering similar to its Sunni Arab cousin. Another dangerous Kurdish group, the Tawheed (meaning "belief in one God") were headquartered further south in Irbil and had been known to commit violent acts against foreigners.

Of course, Kurds exploit other Kurds, lie and cheat for a variety of purposes just like people in every other culture. Americans sometimes lower their guard because of their fondness for the Kurdish people and that could prove a deadly mistake. One incident played out something like the following.

Two Arab-American terps visited me to report encountering an odd incident that deeply troubled them. Both complained about a Kurdish shop owner on base that had video taped them and a few other terps a few nights before. Naturally, terps are protective of their identity, particularly careful not to expose themselves to local nationals who might betray them, resulting in possible injury or death. Popular locally, the shop owner, Hawaz, operated a kind of convenience store, complete with mock 7-11 sign, next to a housing area for troops and civilian contractors. He sold illegal copies of movies and an assortment of trinkets. Young and friendly (only 23 years old), he embraced the chance to own this profitable store within the safety of the base.

Terps often congregated at Hawaz's store in the evenings as friends to talk and watch movies. Hawaz spoke Arabic, Kurdish and a little English. Abdullah was a terp well known to me; a round middle-aged man from Lebanon, we had worked together several times in the past. He hesitated to tell me of the incident but remained troubled by what had happened. Abdullah and his coworker Ekan said that the previous Friday they had observed Hawaz with a video camera while visiting the room of another terp named Curly. Not long after arriving in the room, Hawaz, who had been sleeping on the spare bunk, woke up and began practicing with his new video camera. Playfully, Hawaz began video taping several linguists that were all visiting Curly at the time. Another terp named Nick, objected and sternly demanded Hawaz stop taping and ordered him to erase his picture. Hawaz smiled and waved him off saying it was no problem. Abdullah and Ekan were uncomfortable that Hawaz even possessed a video camera since he was not authorized. In fact, no foreign nationals were allowed still cameras or videos on post. Hawaz told the group not to worry, that he was taking the camera to Dohuk to his friend, as if that would comfort

206

the terps. Abdullah also noted that Hawaz appeared to be living in Curly's room, another violation of base policy.

I promised to look into the matter and began by checking with Hawaz's sponsor. Now this should have been easy as every local national (LN) on post must have a military sponsor whose responsibility it is to vouch for the LN and keep track of his activity in the interest of all our safety. When I visited the Army helicopter squadron listed with Force Protection as the official sponsor, no one knew anything about it. Finally, someone suggested that the squadron was Hawaz's old sponsor but the unit had rotated back to the U.S. and never cleared the paperwork for Hawaz. So in essence, Hawaz was living and working on base without any supervision. Another person in the squadron suggested asking the first sergeant, who admitted knowing Hawaz but remembered that Hawaz had recently left on a trip for Dohuk to buy new supplies for his store and had no idea when Hawaz would return.

Eventually, I tracked down Curly assigned to the MAF Pedestrian Gate, translating for soldiers processing foreign nationals entering the base from Sugar Beet Road. Curly claimed he had been working on FOB MAF for about four months. He admitted his friendship with Hawaz and that Hawaz sometimes slept in his room, which was located less than 100 feet from Hawaz's store. Curly allowed Hawaz to leave his clothes and personal items in his room. In the morning, Curly routinely dropped off the key to his room with Hawaz and reclaimed it in the evening following work. A very friendly gesture but against regulations, effectively allowing a LN almost unlimited, undetected and protected run of the base. Curly discussed the incident spoken of by Ekan and Abdullah, explaining that on that night another interpreter, Nick, had bought Hawaz a video camera from the Post Exchange (PX) and Hawaz video taped a few terp friends who were visiting Curly's room. Curly also remembered that Hawaz eventually took the video camera with him when he left for Dohuk. After further prodding, Curly recalled that as recently as four to five days prior, he saw Hawaz with a digital camera. Hawaz snapped Curly's picture and digitally saved it. He remembered that, at the time, the camera was kept in Hawaz's convenience store. Curly recalled how Hawaz was fascinated with electronic technology and liked to buy the latest gadgets.

Unfortunately for him, LN's were prohibited from buying, owning, or possessing these items on base and could not legally shop in the PX. Curly believed Nick bought Hawaz the digital camera, as well as the video camera. He thought Nick worked with the Military Police unit on FOB MAF. Curly added that Nick was Kurdish like Hawaz, but also spoke Arabic and English. Reluctantly, Curly admitted that he knew Hawaz was not allowed to possess a video camera and told Hawaz so, but did not report the incident to military authorities because he did not know he was supposed to report these types of incidents to anyone. He complained that no one had ever sat down with him and explained what types of incidents to report. A likely story I thought sarcastically, but at the same time in these lax conditions, much of it could easily be true. Terps needed training in several security-related areas but it was just not the Army's priority at the time.

Curly claimed that Hawaz recently took to sleeping in the convenience store and had not slept in Curly's room for some time and admitted the video camera or the digital camera could be among Hawaz's belongings still stored in his room but did not know for certain because he never looked through Hawaz's belongings.

Curly confirmed that several interpreters met at the 7-11 in the evenings as friends to talk and watch movies. As Curly began to relax he started remembering other details of importance. Curly thought it strange that Hawaz's brother, Jim, had a CAC card, which surprised several interpreters and raised special concern since Jim was a LN contractor. A DOD (Department of Defense) Common Access Card, CAC Card as it is known, served as the identification card for all U.S. personnel. For a local national to have one meant trouble as it would provide access to any U.S. installation in Iraq, in fact to any in the world. The CI implications of these two brothers were mounting.

So far we had discovered a Kurdish businessman who had managed to gain permanent access to an important military installation, even so far as opening a business there, without proper documentation or continued supervision. In addition, he had co-opted U.S. sleeping quarters for his personal use, convinced U.S. personnel to buy him illegal photographic equipment with which he took unauthorized pictures of key personnel and possibly other sensitive facilities on the base. This concerned me because his store sat directly across the street from the flight line making it easy for him to videotape aircraft coming and going while remaining concealed in his shop. He had since fled to the north with all the incriminating evidence. His brother also obtained access to the base and all other military installations via an unauthorized Department of Defense ID card. If Hawaz or his brother were connected to the insurgency, then the bad guys had scored a big one. We needed to get to the bottom of this vulnerability but we had to wait for Hawaz to return. In addition, we identified U.S. terps who either had not been briefed on what suspicious incidents to report or were too lazy to do so.

In the meantime, I searched for Nick who had allegedly given the cameras to Hawaz. Tracking him down at the Military Police Unit, Nick said that he thought well of Hawaz. However, Hawaz had once asked to buy his digital camera, but Nick refused reminding Hawaz that he was not allowed to posses a camera. Nick said that another interpreter, Nicky, actually bought the video camera for Hawaz. Nick was sure that Nicky worked for the Civilian Police Advisory Training Team (CPATT) but had since returned to America about one month before for surgery and would not return to Iraq for several months.

Nick complained that Hawaz's brother Jim possessed a CAC card and it made him uncomfortable knowing that a foreign national had access to the dining facility where only months before a suicide bomber had killed so many people. It made me uneasy too because since the bombing, Force Protection had instituted numerous measures to secure the dining facility against foreigners, but a CAC Card would bypass everything because it established the person carrying it was American.

A few weeks later, while driving by the convenience store, we noticed that Hawaz had returned. We immediately interviewed the young man who brazenly denied everything pertaining to video, still pictures, sleeping in Curly's room or any other wrongdoing. We had searched the store and Curly's room but found nothing. The most we could do was ban Hawaz from the base. It wasn't until we talked to his brother Jim that we found something more interesting.

When we finally caught up with Jim he became indignant when we seized his CAC card. Jim said he had been issued the card as part of his contract with U.S. Forces. We were quite surprised to learn that the card identified this Iraqi national as a GS-15 equivalent contractor. General Schedule (GS) is the rank system for U.S. government civilians; GS-1 is the lowest and GS-15 the highest rank possible. Some compare GS-15 to a military equivalent of Colonel. The card listed a fraudulent Social Security number and even afforded him Geneva Convention protection. For an Iraqi national to obtain this kind of access to military installations in a war zone was unthinkable. How could this happen?

It turned out that Jim supplied vehicles to U.S. Forces through the FOB MAF contracting office. As a contractor he supplied FOBs Sykes, Freedom, MAF, Marez and Camp Victory, Baghdad. The clincher for us was that Jim admitted using his CAC card to enter the DFAC on FOB MAF (the one blown up by an Iraqi) without being searched, but tried to console me by claiming he did not use the DFAC much.

Determined to get to the bottom of this vulnerability we headed for the contracting office to talk to the LTC in charge. At first he too was indignant. He said he did not see what the big deal was. He issued the CAC cards as incentives, bragging that he even stipulated the cards in their government contracts to make it legal.

We patiently explained to the LTC that by possessing a CAC card, Jim had access to all facilities without being searched as it created the false impression that he was American. In fact, his CAC card could allow him access to DOD facilities worldwide and Jim had told us of trips to Germany, England and Turkey. His stated rank listed on the card would authorize him additional privileges like priority housing, priority air transportation and others, ahead of all U.S. personnel below his false rank. The LTC still did not budge. Sometimes when people make a mistake they become defensive instead of trying to fix their error. I cleared the room and had a talk with the LTC one on one. I explained that God forbid, if something were to happen, it would be indefensible that he gave a foreign national a CAC card which allowed him access

212

without search, as if he were American. If someone he had issued a CAC to would walk into a dining hall and blow themselves up, or give the card to another person who did so, the entire military establishment would be looking for the idiot who let this happen. I told the LTC that they would crucify him. On top of the pile of evidence against him would be that lonely report I was about to write that said I warned the contracting office and this particular U.S. military officer of the possible consequences of issuing CAC cards to foreign nationals but he refused to heed the warnings. In effect, he would be alone out there, his career and future life on the line. Was he ready to risk that for a foreign national he did not even know and whose brother had just been banned from the base for taking unauthorized photos of personnel and other illegal activity? The LTC's face flushed. He immediately agreed to downgrade Jim's CAC Card to an FOB security badge, but the larger question remained. How many other Iraqi nationals had obtained similar access here and on other installations? If this clause existed in contracting, was security considered during its creation? Obviously not!

We sent a letter to higher command outlining the vulnerability and asking what they knew of this problem at their level, but like so many issues it never was answered.

This case was not the only one of its kind. It did not take long for another Turkish contractor to surface that had been issued a CAC Card with the rank of SES 2. Senior Executive Service (SES) is the General Officer equivalent of government civilians. This foreigner had used his unauthorized rank to obtain personal U.S. Army helicopter transportation around Iraq. By the time it was called to our attention he had been traveling around for some time, shouldering out military personnel with official needs and using the transportation for his personal business. He initially denied any wrongdoing but further inquiry revealed he had acquired the card through the contracting office with the help and recommendation of our old friend General Saladin. The Turkish contractor had toured Saladin around Istanbul and reportedly developed close working relations with him. To me it represented just another shady criminal activity Saladin was tied to and that certain military officials refused to take action on.

17 INSURGENT CELL LEADER

Every morning I read the message traffic on the SIPRNet[16] before starting my day. One day, as I fired up the classified computer system, I scanned the intelligence summaries known as INTSUMs. Not much more than usual. It told how many IEDs exploded the day before and instances where patrols received fire and so forth. I switched to the section of Intelligence Information Reports (IIRs), scanning down the list of interrogations which included a summary of what information resulted. I noticed one report filed by the Special Forces titled "AIF Cell leader working in Mosul." For an IIR it was quite short, only two lines. "AIF Cell leader believed working in Mosul area. Kurdish male, about 30 years old, who goes by name of Salim or Qasim." Great, I thought. That narrows it down to only about 1,000 Kurds that we know of. Others who come and go under escort don't even appear in our database. The names themselves were next to useless. Insurgents

---

[16] SIPRNet - Secret Internet Protocol Router Network is a classified computer network for military personnel.

215

generally use fake names and with the ease of obtaining fake Ids, they can change them frequently. Even if the names were real, we did not know if it was his given name, father's name or grandfather's name. It was worse than a needle in a haystack but that's what we get paid for, finding such needles. I couldn't just let the message slide. For as little information as there was, at least there was something. I walked over to Force Protection and talked to Major White.

"Yeah we saw it in the traffic. What a piece of shit message. Nothing in it. Those guys know nothing about law enforcement or catching bad guys." Major White always cut straight to the point.

Laughing, I suggested, "I know, but we have a kernel of information here. We need to do something."

He was always gung-ho and immediately gave it to Sergeant Allen for distribution to all gates. "Put out a BOLO on this guy," he snapped. "You never know, we might catch this little shit."

I left satisfied we had done what we could. In a perfect world, Special Forces should have brought the info to Force Protection and worked with us to try to narrow down a few suspects. Three things worked against us. First, Special Forces didn't like to work with regular army. They considered themselves elite. Second, they didn't work issues on post, it was out of their lane. Thirdly, they were not investigators. Special Forces liked to move on actionable intelligence and conduct a raid capturing or killing insurgents. They were not about digging around looking for clues. The bureaucracy was not on our side. As crazy as it seems, even within the army all elements do not work together.

The following day, we got a huge breakthrough. A sharp young sergeant at the Pedestrian Gate actually read the BOLO (be on lookout) and had detained two Kurdish males as they entered. Sergeant Parks noticed the name, Salim Habib. Scanning the date of birth she noticed 1976. Bingo!! He matched what little info we had given her. The other man traveled with Salim as a driver; both were connected to the gravel contract on base. Thanks to that very alert gate guard, we were able to spot and eventually neutralize an insurgent cell leader with access to the base. I received a call on my radio while I was driving on the other side of base.

"Phoenix 4, Phoenix 4, Phoenix Base over," my call sign jarred my thoughts as I didn't receive many calls.

"Go ahead Base," I answered.

"Return to Base Phoenix, we have something for you."

"Roger, I am on my way, Phoenix 4 out," I said as I wheeled the vehicle around.

Within about 10 minutes I pulled up to the concrete building Force Protection used as a base, Major White and Sgt. Allen stood outside waiting for me, White grinning from ear to ear.

"Well, Rick, we picked up two guys at the Pedestrian Gate this morning. One of them matches the description of the AIF in that message yesterday," Major White informed me.

I was stunned. "You're kidding, right?" I said enthusiastically.

"No man, it's the real deal. Maybe we got something here. Sgt Bush is bringing them over now. Do your stuff man. Keep me informed," said Major White.

Now it was getting exciting. As I walked across the sand to my compound, I started reviewing all we knew so far, which wasn't much. As soon as I stepped into my office I pulled up the message from the day before. Yeah not much in there, I pretty much had that memorized. I pulled up the data on Salim in BATS. Yeah, he passed a pretty perfunctory interview at Camp Courage. Nothing much out of the ordinary there. Not long after, Sgt. Bush showed up with the two men in handcuffs. Immediately, we processed both men in with new fingerprints, photos and eye scans. I assigned two interpreters Sami and Ali to collect the basic bio data that would form the basis of my interview. Both spoke Kurdish and Arabic, Sami also spoke Turkish.

We interviewed his buddy Ahmad first. Ahmad did not know Salim well but knew one of Salim's younger brothers. They lived in adjoining villages. Salim ran a trucking company that delivered various items to the base. When one of his drivers quit unexpectedly, Salim's brother asked Ahmad if he could drive. Ahmad quickly took the job hauling gravel from Akra to the base in a 35-truck convoy even though it was notoriously dangerous work because insurgents often attacked convoys supplying U.S. Forces.

Ahmad cooperated from the beginning and willingly provided all he knew about Salim and his family, as well as background information about himself that we could verify. Ahmad told us that he saw Salim's brother Nazad on TV as a terrorist. At that time the Iraqis produced a hugely popular news drama program called *Terror in the Grip of Justice* which featured real terrorists soon after capture, admitting their crimes and describing their most heinous acts. The average citizen was at once dumbfounded and spellbound. They saw the insurgents for what they really were, thugs, crooks, opportunists and criminals deserving neither of respect nor sympathy.

Salim also cooperated in the interview. He was small of stature with thick black hair that stood almost taller than he did. Quiet and polite, Salim told us of his trucking company and his work delivering gravel to the Combat Support Battalion on MAF. Smart enough to provide the exact story he had provided in his initial screening, he showed no signs of deception. However, armed with the information Ahmad had provided we knew that Salim had another brother that was already in jail as a captured insurgent. When recording Salim's relatives, he failed to disclose that brother, not knowing what we knew. So now we knew Salim was lying. We just needed to flush out the depth of the deception. Of course, some might find it natural to lie about a brother who was a terrorist. Salim probably believed he would not have received the contract had anyone known about Nazad from the beginning. Iraqis do not understand, nor believe, that Americans do not necessarily hold relatives accountable for the sins of their family. Of course Saddam did. He would have punished or maybe killed all the immediate family in a case like this and Salim had lived under that threat. If Salim had been forthcoming about his brother and had disavowed any connection with him, we might have believed him and kept him under observation but allowed him to continue working with restricted access because he supplied something of dire need to the military, gravel. The rainy season was approaching fast and Mosul would soon turn into a huge mud hole. Base officials ordered thousands of tons of gravel to shore up roads and areas surrounding the airfield. But Salim chose to lie about his brother and that is never received well. He didn't just forget about the brother either. He was asked specifically whether he had any other brothers and sisters. Salim said, "No."

Finding an insurgent among thousands of simple workers is often compared to finding a needle in a haystack. If you looked for a needle in a haystack, not knowing if one actually existed, you would likely give up after a short while. But if you looked for the needle, knowing it was in there somewhere, then you would not stop until you found it. You would focus all your energy until you found it. That's what this situation reminded me of. We knew Salim was dirty, we just needed to prove it. That wouldn't be easy.

While Salim rested in the holding cell, we visited the unit that had written the original intelligence report to try and learn more information. The officer in charge, CW4 Massey, was surprised to see us. When we told him we had picked up the man in the report he was taken aback. "I didn't know anyone paid attention to our reports," he said with a smile.

"When it comes to the safety of the base, we absolutely pay attention," I countered. "The good news is we have your man in custody."

Massey was stunned. "What? That's great. You guys are sharp over there."

I thanked him but held up my hand to say there was more. "The bad news is there was little information of value in your report and we don't have much to go on. I need more information. Do you know anything else you can tell us?"

Unfortunately, Massey didn't have any additional information at that time. He agreed to task his sources for more details but that would take time. I reminded him that time was of the essence if we wanted to keep him detained. Massey promised to make it a priority.

Meanwhile, we started calling in all 35 truck drivers for interview. Most of them lived in or around the village of Salim. We labored under the hope that each would provide little pieces of the puzzle, not just about Salim's brother but about Salim's relations and contacts with his brother. Individually, none of them knew much but between all of them we were able to piece together strong evidence that Salim and his brother were working together against Coalition Forces.

Later, Massey confirmed through his sources that Salim was wanted by Iraqi forces for involvement with his brother. That was important but we needed to find out Salim's efforts against us before turning him over to the Iraqis. Once in their hands we might never learn the details of the two brothers' operation or uncover others with access to our bases who might be working with them.

We brought Salim back in for questioning; this time he was not so calm. A night in the BIF had caused some introspection. He realized his interview was not as routine as we had originally contended.

Salim immediately began objecting, politely, "Why am I being held? Have I done something wrong?" We left the goggles on as we talked this time.

"You have not been entirely truthful with us Salim. We trusted you and you have violated that trust." I circled Salim as I spoke and he tried to follow my voice by turning his head.

"What have I been untruthful about? I swear by Allah that I have told the truth," his voice still timid.

"Are you a good Muslim?" I asked.

"Yes, yes," he answered quickly.

"Then why do you anger Allah by lying to us right now?"

"I do not lie to you, how have I lied?" he objected.

"We asked you if you had any other brothers and sisters and you did not tell us about Nazad," I said.

"Nazad is not my brother," again responding without thinking. "I disowned him when he was arrested for terrorism. I am an honest businessman risking my life to help U.S. Forces. Why do you treat me this way?"

Salim had been trained well. He was taught not to confront interrogators if caught but to continue to feign cooperation, win them over. Raise doubt about their information. It is a useful technique. Americans in general do not follow-up well. If a suspect can raise doubt about their information Americans will often soften, because our culture is the opposite of the one he grew up in. In America, we believe it better to let 100 guilty men go free than to convict one innocent man. Saddam would have said, better to convict 100 innocent people than to allow one guilty man to go free.

"Really? Tell us more about your brother and how you disowned him," I encouraged him.

Salim paused then began slowly, "When the police arrested Nazad he was shown on TV as a criminal. He disgraced our entire family. None of us would have anything to do with him from that day."

Unfortunately for him, we had intelligence that Salim had been in contact with his brother through a third party. We would not let Salim off so easy and continued to pressure him but he would not break. We suspected he would use the access of the trucking company to take some action against us but we did not have enough time to find out. Another agency decided to take Salim off our hands. We never found out any more about him. Just to be sure, Force Protection had increased the inspection of the trucks entering the base. This proved time consuming and caused traffic jams at the gates between the two posts that irritated everyone on base. However, it may have paid off.

18 POSSIBLE VBIED?

It began as a crazy day. Late the previous night, two truck drivers brought in a load of gravel and hidden inside the dump trucks were 24 propane tanks. It could have made a heck of a VBIED. The term refers to Vehicle Borne Improvised Explosive Device. Once again, alert gate guards discovered the tanks almost by accident. The tanks did not show up on the x-ray conducted just inside the gate. The gravel had masked the tanks well. They would have passed through undetected but the tanks had jiggled around during the trip and parts of them became exposed. An alert guard happened to look in the back, saw the tips of a few propane tanks and ordered a full inspection. Could this have been what Salim was up to? Testing how to bring a few high-powered explosives onto the base? Was this a test run? Had others already made it through? The next morning, we interviewed the two persons who originally ordered the propane, both were Turkish hadji shop owners on base. They swore that they just ordered it from a man named Kemal up in Zahko. Kemal had rented the trucks, hired the drivers and bought the goods. When we interviewed the drivers of the truck with the propane, we discovered that one of them had been kicked off the base before for smuggling. I remembered him because he was the

225

crybaby. He cried from the moment we took him into custody; I don't think he ever stopped crying. As a grown man it looked terrible for him. The crybaby had a partner driving with him. Both were transferred to the BIF for interrogation. Their stories were weak but with no evidence to show any intent beyond smuggling, they all escaped prison again and were banned from the base. The Turks who had ordered the propane were kicked out of the country.

Ramazan

Everyday was filled with new cases to investigate but we were not manned fully enough to take care of them, operating at 30% of our manpower allotment. Mosul was like the Barbary Coast, a pirates' den of crooks and thieves all trying to take advantage of U.S. Forces. Under the guise of supplying or helping the troops, the chaos worked to the advantage of the insurgents. Criminal elements can develop knowledge or methods of advantage to the insurgency. It's difficult enough warding off the criminal elements while searching for insurgents but it is worse when our own side wittingly or unwittingly helps the enemy effort.

Word reached me that Ramazan, a known criminal, had regained access to the base. I had to think hard when I heard the name. Ramazan was a man we had barred from the base months before, how could he have returned? This time he had been detained in a random search at West Gate and the guards radioed me to come check it out. As I approached the car, Ramazan was a passenger in the back seat and next to him sat an American already with his military ID card shoved out the window for me to see.

"Lt. Col. Wilcox," he said. "Retired Army Special Forces, let us pass," he yelled out the window.

Ramazan recognized me immediately and smiled while flashing a military dependent ID. I had to chuckle at the Colonel because I almost could not believe what I saw.

"Where did you get this ID Card Ramazan?" I suspected it must be a fake but I underestimated my old nemesis.

Still smiling he answered, "When I went back to Turkey I met a nice American girl at the base and we just got married."

I couldn't believe it. What stupid young girl could meet this crook and in a few months marry him, then watch him run back to Iraq to try to extort more money.

Turning to the Colonel, "What is your business here," I asked curtly "and what are you doing with Ramazan?" The Colonel looked surprised as if no one had questioned him before.

"I am a contractor and Ramazan works for me," he said impatiently.

"Is that right? Well you both will have to follow this officer back to Force Protection for a little discussion," I told him.

The Colonel objected but had no choice in the matter. Major White had been listening on the radio and was waiting in his office for the Colonel to show up. In the meantime, I asked my office to run a background check on Ramazan, but par for the BATS system, nothing showed up. No photo, fingerprints, data—nothing. It was incredible but just another example of the problems with BATS. I sent Ramazan under escort to have his fingerprints and photo processed again into BATS while I went with the Colonel to see Major White. Ramazan had miscalculated once again. In any other country, his military dependent ID would have gained him access to a military base but this was Iraq. Dependents are not authorized in the war zone. His card carried no privileges here unless the Commander specifically authorized them, and the Commander had made no such authorization.

Short and a bit overweight, the Colonel sat in White's office and started off with his resume in the Special Forces and how important he was. He continued, "Ramazan works for me and I vouch for him 100%. He is a good guy and there should be no problem with him having access under my escort." White let him ramble a few minutes but was losing patience fast.

I got the look that I should say something before White lost his temper so I asked the Colonel, "How long have you known Ramazan?"

Sitting back in the worn out chair he thought a moment, "Well, I met him a few weeks back in Dohuk and we hit it off. He is a great guy."

Now, I started to lose my temper just a little. "Did you know he was deeply involved in the crime syndicate here in Iraq and had been banned from all bases in the country? In fact, he was sent back to Turkey and should not even be in Iraq right now. Did you know that your association with him now casts suspicion on you and your eligibility to remain in this country under contract with the U.S. Government? Did you bother to check into his background at all before hiring him or transporting him around the country, using your rank to shelter a known criminal?" The Colonel looked flabbergasted.

White leaned forward in his chair now and laid into Wilcox, "I should have both of you thrown off the base. Ramazan is bad news and you trying to bring him on a military installation is serious business."

Wilcox was scared. Gone was the swagger of throwing around his former rank that had apparently allowed him to bully his way through similar situations. "Now fellas, listen, I didn't know about this guy's background. He means nothing to me. I have a job to do. I really need to get going. You guys do whatever you think is right with Ramazan. Sorry for the misunderstanding." Wilcox talked with White a few more minutes then was off like a rocket. Shortly after, soldiers escorted Ramazan over to the Force Protection office where we met again outside.

"Well it almost worked Ramazan, you thought you had it made this time," I said.

Ramazan, looked around for his friend. "Where is Colonel Wilcox?" he asked sheepishly.

"Oh he left so fast he couldn't say good-bye. No, you are on your own my friend and that means you belong to me once again." Ramazan's shoulders slumped. He knew the outcome. White had him scheduled for the next convoy to the border with Turkey. "If you come back again we will throw you in jail. Your last warning Ramazan." Somehow I didn't think he would heed that warning.

As I said, it is hard enough keeping foreign criminals out of Iraq without former U.S. military officers who should know better contributing to the problem.

19 MOLE AMONG PRISON TERPS

A tremendous break in information came our way and we decided to jump on it. For months, rumors circulated among base employees and even a few prisoners that an interpreter within the DIF, located on MAF, was providing intelligence to the insurgency—in effect, a mole within our own prison. Now we had solid source information that the rumors were true. In another location, a captured insurgent had confessed to receiving information indirectly from a source inside the DIF. The insurgent did not know exactly who it was and had never seen the person or heard a name, but knew it was an interpreter. The insurgents were smart enough to compartmentalize their information so no one person could compromise much if captured. Still, we had a nugget of info that narrowed the field somewhat.

That no one took interest in following up on the rumors was one thing, but still no one seemed interested in pursuing this solid lead. Actionable intelligence to most military meant something like, "Ahmed, an insurgent, is meeting in such and such house tonight at 6:30, capture him." Units loved to conduct raids and sweeps looking for people or weapons but few wanted to do the traditional gumshoe-type investigating needed to ferret out true spies. If it wasn't handed to them on a silver platter, they didn't touch it. Most didn't know what to do with such information anyway but that was beside the point. I expected MI to jump on this type of lead but MI always seemed engaged in other tasks. No other group was capable of taking on such a hunt.

Luckily for our side, Major White was hot for the challenge. He could not abide the thought of an infiltrator in the base prison providing intelligence endangering the lives of all of us, including the Iraqi interpreters so vital to the mission.

A mole in the prison could provide names of persons captured and what information they gave to U.S. Forces. He could compromise critical details of the interrogation process and how to resist it. He might also reveal names and descriptions of interpreters working for U.S. Forces who could then be threatened or killed. Sometimes, the insurgency could convince an interpreter to work for them in exchange for him and his family staying alive.

White encouraged us to hunt this mole and we were all for it. After all, this is what counterintelligence is all about and we wanted to crack this case as soon as possible. Unfortunately, the task was daunting. There were more than a score of interpreters and they remained engaged 12 hours a day. The units did not want to free them up for our interviews, which could take several hours. White took care of that part. He arranged mandatory interviews for all the interpreters in the DIF under the guise of periodic security re-screening. This was important for two reasons; first, we didn't want to alert the terps that we were mole hunting and second, it precluded excuses for not appearing before us.

A look at the roster of terps discouraged some in my office. There were too many possible suspects. Figuring about three hours for each one, just the preliminary interviews would take more than a week. We had to schedule these interviews in our spare time as the regular daily work of screenings and crisis response had to continue. Some of the terps were on leave and would not return for a month. Reasonably calculating the time to conduct the first round of interviews we came up with about a month. That seems too long to allow an informant to continue within our midst but it was that or nothing. No one else was doing anything. We would have to squeeze it in as a special project.

Looking down the list with our crack analyst Hiram Dahmer, we noticed four groups of terps. First we had a few Assyrian Christians, second were Kurdish Christians, third came the Arab Christians and finally the Arab Sunni Muslims. No Shiite terps were employed.

All of our terps were highly educated for Iraqis. At a minimum all were high school graduates, most had at least some college. Several had graduated college, and a few had advanced degrees in English, government or law. One had been trained as an engineer.

For security purposes, almost all of the terps used an American first name on the job and with each other. As I mentioned before, terps were rightfully scared of revealing too much about their real identity because they knew better than anyone that no one could be trusted. They lived with the daily fear that if one of them was a bad guy, their very lives and families could be in danger.

We began calling them in one by one to verify their original personal information provided upon employment and to quiz them about other terps among them. Personal quirks, tidbits of background and even insights of colleagues that might be acting suspicious, all proved valuable to the overall effort. Each terp provided a few pieces to a puzzle but no grand picture had yet formed. Some actively worried about the possibility of a traitor among them. As we had predicted, the initial interviews took us over a month to complete. After charting out all our potential leads and additional questions we had narrowed the field to three persons that we wanted to further scrutinize in a second round of questioning. These three all had unanswered areas of their past that we wanted to pursue. In addition, we could not discount the idea that there could be more than one bad guy among the terps.

The first of the three, Scott was a Yezidi, an obscure Kurdish religion of northern Iraq and a few other border areas. I studied a little about the Yezidi religion because I found it so interesting. Not far from Mosul is the small town of Bashika, a bastion of Yezidis and many of their sect came to work for U.S. Forces. They are often misunderstood and were severely persecuted under Saddam and later by radical Muslims. This persecution continued long after I left and turned quite brutal. In April 2007, radical Islamists stopped a bus filled with Christians and Yezidis. After checking IDs they asked the Christians to get off the bus, then drove 23 Yezidi passengers to a place in Mosul and executed them. Some suspected the execution was in retaliation for the stoning of a Yezidi woman who had converted to Islam not long before. This type of violence has gone back and forth for some time.

One core Yezidi belief involves the notion that Satan is a fallen angel but later reconciled with God. One Yezidi explained this belief derived from the book of Job where Satan is talking with God but I am not sure of the accuracy of the characterization. Anyway, Muslims look at this view of Satan as heresy and a form of devil worship, although Yezidis do not believe in the devil. Yezidis harbor some other strange beliefs centered in nature. They also avoid the color blue but I could not find a Yezidi who actually knew why. Less than one million Yezidis exist worldwide, mostly in southeastern Turkey and northern Iraq. Locals like them and think they are good people, honest and fairly devout in their morals. I have interviewed dozens of Yezidis and they seem simple and honest, but their core beliefs are somewhat strange. One cannot convert to the religion but must be born into it. At any rate, they are a people who want to be left to worship God in their own way. This is not accepted well in Iraq. Many are shunned and face difficulty finding jobs. They throng to the safety of U.S. Forces where they

235

are treated kindly. They are willing to perform any type of labor and some know enough English to translate.

Scott cooperated fully and we soon downgraded him from the suspicious list. The other two were not so simple. Frank, a 45-year old Arab, had been working as a terp at the DIF for about a year. He claimed to have been threatened when an unknown person slipped a note under his door promising to kill his wife and family if he did not stop working for U.S. Forces. His wife had picked up the letter and became frightened. Frank claimed that three of his friends received similar letters around the same time, adding that his friend Rahid saw Frank's name on a kind of hit list posted in a local mosque. Out of fear, Frank and his friends decided to quit working for several months. After almost six months, with money running low, Frank and his friends decided to return to work for U.S Forces.

Frank's story was all too familiar among terps. Just about all had claimed threats of some kind. A portion of the threats were valid, but some were designed to win sympathy or add credibility to their loyalties. In Frank's case the cover story had a few holes. When questioned about the threatening letter, Frank stumbled in the explanation of details and when asked to produce the letter or a copy, suddenly he remembered that in a fit of anger he destroyed it, conveniently destroying the only evidence that it ever existed. Once again, we wanted to conduct a surprise interview of his wife which might have shed some light on the veracity of the facts, but we were not allowed.

Another point of interest lay in the list on the wall in the mosque. Imagine your name is on a hit list posted on a wall. Frank supposedly forgot to ask Rahid the name of the mosque, where it was, who else was on the list and the final kicker, Frank could not remember Rahid's full name, making it impossible to verify any aspect of this tale.

Frank claimed he graduated Mosul University with a B.A. in English translation. He stated that while in school, Baath Party officials made him join the Party or face expulsion. Frank relented but stayed at the Muayyid Level (sympathizer), never attending meetings or participating in Baath Party activities. Following college, he joined the Iraqi Army as a Lieutenant serving as a communications officer for nine years. Frank was eventually selected to serve for the UN Iran-Iraq Observer Group moving around the country under the supervision of an Iraqi Colonel for three years. After that, he transferred back to his old unit and claimed he never fought in Desert Storm.

Doubts lingered about Frank's history when he stated he never met or was debriefed by any Iraqi Intelligence officers during his time in the Army. It was hard to believe Frank was only one of six translators picked for a sensitive UN mission and was never exploited by Iraqi intelligence. We suspected once again that Frank was less than truthful, but we had no authority to verify the facts. As an Assyrian Christian, we didn't think he would likely be accepted into the insurgency but he could have been co-opted by

237

them under threat, or he could have been lying about his Christian background. He provided the name of his church but again, we were prevented from checking out these details, which could have helped exonerate or convict Frank.

For the next ten years Frank claimed he drove a taxi all over Mosul, yet he could not name one other taxi driver, claiming he kept to himself. Ten years driving a taxi and can't name one other driver? Frank's story cried out with warning signs and we were anxious to pin him down, on these questions. However, the other suspect, David, was equally interesting.

David stood only five and a half feet tall and gave the impression to everyone that he was a sneaky and aggressive person. When initially interviewed for employment, he provided a similar story as Frank. His family was threatened, he quit work for a few months then returned and then he drove a taxi for a while—details we didn't notice until charting and comparing interviews. He differed in that he never served in the military and was trained as a nurse. This was all interesting because David was originally assigned to the hospital as a translator. One would think a trained medical professional would want to work in the hospital, but not David. His coworkers told us he lobbied hard to transfer to the prison. He told several people in the hospital he did not like it there and astutely worked the system to transfer to the prison the first chance that became available. The prison is not usually the first choice of assignment for terps. First of all, it is dangerous because

238

you come into contact with insurgents who if released, can reveal your identity and have you killed. Secondly, the prison is a dirty, stinky place compared to a hospital. You are around the lowest of people who at any moment could lunge out and harm you. While you also sometimes deal with insurgents in the hospital, for the most part you are dealing with Iraqi citizens and are helping people in pain often from injury suffered at the hands of terrorists. The environment is good and even the food is better. The hospital is a coveted assignment so we remained curious why David fought to transfer to the prison. Obviously, we worried that the insurgents directed him to transfer there to provide better information.

These were some of the questions we wanted to ask David but we didn't get the chance. When we started conducting the mass interviews of terps David always seemed to be unavailable for schedule. Later, he decided to take leave and an inattentive NCO allowed it, even though we had put out the word that no one could take leave until their interview had been completed. David had slipped away on leave and while we waited patiently, it was already a week past his return day and no one had heard from him. He had become hot property on the suspect list and we had given orders to escort him in the moment he showed up.

Another week passed when we received a message from Headquarters that David was in custody and under investigation by another agency in Kirkuk. The other agency asked if we could search David's room and develop evidence to support their investigation.

Happy that he was in custody we jumped on the matter. The Base Commander authorized the search of his room on MAF. We didn't find much of value at first—a copy of his Iraqi ID card, a few contact numbers of friends, a poem he wrote. But then we found a few more interesting items including unit training plans and communication signs, neither of which he should have had in his possession let alone kept hidden in his room. If he had been tasked to translate them, which he hadn't, there was no need to conceal them. We also found some drugs and syringes which were not U.S. but came from the Iraqi market. None of these items were the nail in his coffin, so to speak, but they helped in his subsequent conviction.

Through further investigation we found other reasons to remove Frank from his position in the DIF so we were more confident that, at least for the time being, the mole in the prison was resolved.

20 FENCE THIEVES

A little fear of punishment was enough to break him.

Fear is a powerful motivator that, if used properly, can turn the tide in interrogations. Fear can appear in several forms. It can be created in the mind of the suspect in varying degrees by logic, environment and even threats. Threats in particular are a tool the political left wishes to take away from interrogators. Some argue that certain threats, such as the threat of physical harm or death is torture. The threat of physical harm can be more powerful, and thus more useful, than the actual harm itself. Saddam's henchmen enjoyed beating prisoners, but even they learned that after a time, a prisoner becomes hardened to beatings and just learns to endure them. Others say the cultural concept of fatalism sets in and the prisoner just accepts his fate, rendering beatings almost no value. Regardless of Saddam's strategy, and misguided media portrayals, beating a prisoner was never an option for Americans. But Arab fatalism is an important concept that affects interrogation. The object is not to allow the prisoner to slip into fatalistic thoughts or he will give up hope and not provide anything of value, but will instead, shut down and prepare to absorb whatever punishment

241

awaits him. A good interrogator holds out the possibility of dire consequence with the hope that the suspect can alter the course with the truth. Provide an out to the prisoner. Give him the hope that he can emerge with little harm by painting the consequence from telling the truth as better than the alternative.

Honor is the desire not to shame one's family and can be used in interrogation. Honor can only be used against someone who possesses a sense of it. Not everyone does, and a sense of honor differs in degree in each person.

Conversely, in the very beginning of the interrogation process, before any physical pain has been administered, threatening physical harm can create so much fear that the prisoner will cooperate without ever having to inflict harm. Yes, but some argue that you must be able to back up any threats or they do not carry credibility with the prisoner. Once again, it depends on the specific case. Interrogators can convince prisoners they have the will even if in fact they don't. Ruses and trickery are key.

I remember the case of the two Iraqis apprehended cutting away parts of the chain link perimeter fence of our base in Mosul. Force Protection spotted them on the video surveillance cameras. The two perpetrators had done this before but had escaped prior to apprehension. This day we finally caught them. A little context is necessary here because you are probably wondering what kind of perimeter security we had if Iraqis could steal the fence without detection. The base contained miles of perimeter, partly consisting

242

of concrete walls, other parts stretching out into farm fields consisting of two rows of chain link fence. The outer row was left over from the Saddam regime and had fallen into disrepair in places. The second row was built by U.S. forces who continually maintained and monitored it. Saddam's old fence provided an added layer of protection but was not considered critical to our defense. Parts of it had rusted away and sections were missing in certain areas. Our two suspects had taken to cutting away sections, rolling them up and hauling them away to be sold in the market as scrap metal. Had they tried to cut away our interior fence, they could have been shot. The sections they were after existed on the far side of the perimeter obscured partially by terrain and out of the sight of both Towers 23 and 24. Force Protection monitored the area from a surveillance camera only part of the time. Responding to alarms in that area took ten to twenty minutes. On two previous occasions, the suspects drove their sheep into that area and, since they did not see anyone around, took the opportunity to steal a few sections of the fence. By the time our response team arrived they were gone. This time the two got greedy and tried to steal longer sections than in the past, allowing our response team the needed time to surround and capture them. They brought the two hapless herdsmen in for interrogation.

Both were poor ragged shepherds, illiterate and innocent in many ways. Ali Ahmad and Mohanad Mahmood came from the local village known as Abu-Sa'if. We immediately separated them into our jail/makeshift holding area. We made the jail out of a 20-foot shipping container with bars cut in the door so it had the real feel of a jail. We threw in some wooden bunk beds we built and voila—a field jail. Closing the big steel doors and pulling the handle shut made a loud noise that had a psychological effect on prisoners. When those doors shut, it had a scary, permanent sound. Again, the psychology of the process was important. By regulation, we could only keep prisoners in custody for 72 hours then we had to either transfer them to the BIF or set them free. Our BIF was a permanent concrete structure that strictly complied with all DOD regulations for housing prisoners. Our field jail was temporary but served its purpose well. It allowed us to hold prisoners safely without fear of them attacking us or escaping. We had several CI agents and five interpreters including females. Interviews could take hours so others had to be held close by but often without armed guards.

We locked Ali into the jail and took Mohanad first for interrogation. Mohanad was younger and much more frightened by the capture. He repeated several times, "Don't hurt me, I am innocent, don't hurt me I am innocent."

"Innocent of what?" I asked.

"I didn't steal anything," he said.

"Who said you stole something?" I replied. "Just go in that room and sit down." The interpreter motioned toward interrogation room three.

244

I entered the room behind Mohanad and pulled the little metal chair back away from the plywood desk separating us. Suspects sometimes liked to scoot up close to see what notes we took. Even though they could not read them, they would note what questions caused us to write something down. Ali, our interpreter, obtained some basic background information from Mohand before I began the interview. Then we took Mohanad into the processing room for fingerprints, eye scan, and photograph, adding the biometric data to the BATS database. At that time BATS contained a few hundred thousand entries of prisoners, employees and anyone else that had come in contact with Coalition Forces. As mentioned before, if we got a hit on a person that was helpful but if not, we did not assume he was clean, only that we were not able to find out for sure. Mohanad did not show up in the database. A guard escorted him back to the interrogation room where I reviewed the personal data sheet on Mohanad that the interpreter had collected. Entering the room I could see Mohanad was nervous and worried. He was sweating beyond the normal amount expected from the 120-degree heat. Positioned in the chair, he appeared almost like a scared puppy that had been abused by his owner. Every noise or sudden movement caused him to flinch. This exaggerated startled response raised my suspicion that Mohanad had possibly been abused as a child or suffered some other traumatic experience in life.

Let's examine a possible scenario for extracting information from these two men and decide if it should be authorized. Following the initial general questions about his background and family, I asked Mohanad about Ali, trying to obtain information about his partner that might be useful in his subsequent interrogation. Mohanad admitted he did not know Ali well. Ali was a friend of the family, a fellow shepherd that Mohanad had come to know only within the last several months. He told us that Ali was not from Abu-Sa'if village but another one across town. He insisted they both were simple shepherds and had done nothing wrong. For a second, he became bold and demanded to know why he had been detained, that we were violating his rights. Someone must have told him to start demanding things from the Americans to scare them into providing good treatment. I nipped that in the bud by slamming his dossier on the table and coming from behind the desk to stand in front of him.

Towering over him with an angry scowl I said, "You don't have any rights here. You are our prisoner. You will answer our questions and cooperate or you will be punished and jailed. You will in effect disappear." The interpreter kept up simultaneously translating my words.

Mohanad recoiled in the chair frightened and started frantically repeating again, "Don't hurt me, I am innocent, don't hurt me I am innocent." He denied stealing anything or even touching the fence. He said we were mistaken. After 30 minutes or so of this I decided to use a different kind of approach.

I became quiet and sat on the edge of the table facing Mohanad with one leg dangling from the top. Softly, I spoke while looking into his frightened eyes, "It looks as though you continue to refuse to cooperate with me." I began slowly, "Do you know what will happen to you if you continue to resist? You will likely be sent to Abu Ghraib prison." With those words Mohanad straightened in the chair, completely attentive, his head wagging side to side. "Do you know what happens in Abu Ghraib Prison? I just came from there. You will be put in a room about the size of this one." I drew an imaginary square on the ground. "There is a hole in the center of the floor to piss into. The smell is overwhelming and there is no running water. Everyone sleeps on rugs on the cement floor. About 20-25 men share the space, hardened criminals most of whom have not seen a woman in months. You will be put in the middle of them, and when the lights go out at night, YOU will be the woman. They will take turns with you."

Mohanad yelled, "No don't send me to Abu Ghraib prison, I don't want to go to Abu Ghraib prison."

Of course we would not have sent him to Abu G, but Mohanad did not know that. The threat of being sent there was enough to break him. In tears, Mohanad begged, "Tell me what to do. What must I say not to go there."

I answered calmly, "Just tell me the truth, the whole truth, not half lie and half truth. If you convince me, then I will ensure you are not sent to Abu Ghraib." Mohanad shook his head rapidly in agreement.

He began by admitting to stealing sections of fence he later planned to sell in the Babish De'ed market in a downtown Mosul neighborhood. Mohanad stated that it was Ali's idea to steal the fence. Mohanad recounted that approximately two weeks prior, he had witnessed several other individuals, that he did not recognize as anyone from his village, remove part of the perimeter fencing and transport it away in a truck. Mohanad claimed that he informed the Iraqi National Guard (ING) later that same day (this was information we could verify). On the next day, Mohanad received a letter from unknown individuals threatening to behead him if he provided any more information to the ING. Mohanad was scared. Iraqi's who want to trust their police and military knew they could not be trusted as they were corrupt and had been penetrated by the insurgency. Later an individual contacted Mohanad and asked him to work for them stealing sections of fence. Mohanad said he was afraid but agreed. Although he did not know the person's name, Mohanad said the two were scheduled to meet again the next day. Mohanad also admitted being detained approximately two years before by U.S./Coalition forces but insisted that it was a mistake. He was incarcerated for nine days and released (more information we could check).

Ali was a little different, more street savvy, a resident of a small village on the other side of Mosul. At first, he repeatedly denied attempting to steal the perimeter fence stating that he was only walking along the railroad tracks tending his 50 sheep which had freed themselves from enclosed pasturage on his farm.

Lying is the default for most prisoners. It is not looked at as necessarily wrong when done in the service of Allah. Prisoners often say, "I swear by Allah" when they are actually lying. This might be compared to an American saying, "I swear to God I didn't do it." Muslims have told me that a lie can be appropriate if it will achieve good or when the truth might lead to harmful results, especially when dealing with infidels. Just so there is no misunderstanding, Islam forbids lying. The Holy Quran speaks to it in Surah 40: 28 and the Prophet Mohammed spoke to it in the Hadith but that does not stop varying interpretations of others verses that are said to make provision for lying. Abdullah Al Araby wrote of the principle of Al-Takeyya, meaning to prevent, which in a larger sense pertains to permission for Muslims to lie to prevent harm to themselves, to other Muslims or in the broadest sense, if it would prevent harm to Islam.

Without becoming too technical or philosophical, let me say that prisoners almost always lie initially, but that should not discourage an interrogator. In fact, it is helpful especially if the suspect lies about a matter the interrogator already has confirmed. Catching a suspect in a lie provides leverage to the interrogator and can be used to pressure the suspect into eventually confessing the truth.

Because many of the prisoners are what I like to call simple shepherds, they may lie to American interrogators to conceal a horrible life under Saddam. They may have been forced to do things they are not proud of and now seek a chance to change. A man has a right to change his life, to start over with a clean slate. Of course, it is not good to start the clean slate with new lies but an interrogator's task is to distinguish between a person's deceptions.

I remember interviewing a candidate for a translator position with our forces. He hailed from the Al-Jibory tribe, known for its loyalty to Saddam before the war. He claimed his father was persecuted by Saddam and even arrested while working in Syria because he was Iraqi. The son had worked various jobs on post and was liked by the troops. He admitted serving in the elite Adnan Republican guard unit in the engineers but only building bridges. We had to determine if he was lying or sincere. Iraqis are accomplished liars who learned to lie convincingly to survive under Saddam. This is not my assessment, but that of several Iraqis confessing their own faults. It is often difficult to catch them and at the same time a man can change his life, in other words want to live and tell the truth. Under Saddam they had to serve in the military or suffer punishment or even death. We had to determine if their loyalties were and remained with Saddam or they truly were on our side. This was no easy task.

Let us return to Ali. He insisted that his friend Mohanad was too far away for him to see what Mohanad was doing. Ali suggested Mohanad might have been stealing some fence but he knew nothing about it.

Of course, we had his picture on video but did not want to show it to him because it would reveal our ability to monitor that area. Insurgents would sometimes allow themselves to be captured to learn our procedures, methods, strengths and capabilities. In this case, the insurgents may have recruited these two shepherds to steal the fence knowing they would be caught and released, after which they could provide the insurgency with intelligence about our methods and vulnerabilities. Anyway, even if we played the videotape, he would have simply denied it was him, claiming it was merely someone who looked like him.

Ali claimed that "by Allah" he would never steal fence from U.S. Forces and that he had actually been threatened in the past by insurgents for assisting Coalition Forces by reporting unexploded ordinance he found in pastures around his farm. On that very morning, Ali claimed he had informed Ahmet, a local national interpreter of a Striker patrol in the area, of three more pieces of ordinance on his farm. This was valuable because it could be verified if needed. However, it was not necessary because after several more hours of questioning, Ali finally admitted to attempting to steal the fence. He also admitted to being detained by Coalition Forces two years before for other thefts, but spent only a short period in jail before release. Almost comically, Ali said he did not know which jail, as his head was covered during the interviews.

I had to laugh since to some in the liberal community back home, hooding a suspect also constituted torture, surely a remnant of the pictures from Abu Ghraib of the hooded prisoner standing on a box repeatedly shown in the U.S. media.

Hooding is a necessary operational precaution especially when transporting prisoners. Once again, we do not want insurgents to easily learn the locations of interrogation facilities, as they become targets of mortar attack. In addition, the Al Qaeda training manual lists basic information of value to the insurgency including exterior shape, transportation, total area, unit designations, fortifications and tunnels, guard posts, lighting, locations of ammunition storage, vehicles, names, ranks and description of key personnel, communication equipment and other specifics all of which is observable while in custody and moving around the base.

Moreover, beyond operational security, hooding has a profound psychological effect on prisoners. In effect, it scares the crap out of them. Of course it affects some more than others. But for a moment, picture that you are under friendly questioning and you successfully resist. Suddenly, you are hooded from behind and roughly transported to another location where the questioning is a little more rigorous. For some, this relatively minor escalation in tactic is enough to gain cooperation.

Mohanad and Ali's information allowed us to work toward discovering their connection with local insurgent groups, but once again, the scenario raises the question—was scaring Mohanad with

252

the possibility of transfer to Abu Ghraib prison torture? Evaluating this scenario is tricky because the story of what would have happened to Mohanad had he been transferred to Abu Ghraib was fairly accurate. The ruse consisted of the possible transfer to the prison, which considering his offense was unlikely. However, in some people's minds such a ruse would have caused Mohanad to believe there was a threat and that constituted torture. Ridiculous! I believe most Americans would concur that using ruses which include fear, as in the scenario above, are a successful, useful and reliable technique that falls well short of the bar for torture.

21 SUSPICIOUS SYRIAN TRAVEL

Iraqis with access to the base were of the highest security importance to us because as we saw with the suicide bombing of the DFAC in December of 2004, mistakes in this area could be fatal to large numbers of soldiers and civilians. We kept our eyes and ears open for any suspicious activity and sometimes it paid off. An alert sergeant in the Mayor's office alerted us to one such case. In Army terms, the Mayor is the Commander in charge of facilities on the base. He assigns and maintains all the buildings including quarters. A base is like a small town and the Mayor Cell is responsible to make sure it runs smoothly just like a civilian mayor. Within the Mayor Cell is a staff of soldiers responsible for maintenance, administration, and infrastructure. They employ lots of Iraqi labor to perform the more menial tasks, freeing up soldiers for war fighting. On this day, one of the sharp sergeants in the Mayor Cell notified my office that one of his Iraqi employees, Khalif, had just returned from an extensive absence. In fact, he had been away 20 days when he was supposed to be gone only a week. Khalif returned as if nothing happened and no suspicion would have been raised had he notified his supervisor that he needed additional time off or provided a reasonable excuse. Khalif was young and foolish and the whole thing might have been forgotten but this sergeant knew his men and he felt there was something wrong. Khalif was not himself and returned acting strange. The sergeant just asked that we check it out.

Khalif had an interesting background in that in a previous interview, he admitted traveling to Syria in March to search for his father. Khalif convincingly told a sad story of how he had not seen his father in nine years and claimed on that trip he never found him, and did not know where he was living. Khalif's father, Abdul, drove a truck that traveled between Syria, Jordan, Lebanon and Iraq, a dangerous route considering insurgents could attack, hi-jack or rob him at any time.

As the soldiers escorted Khalif into our compound he stopped dead at the T-walled entrance, hesitating to enter. Our small compound was imposing and a reputation among Iraqis developed that it was a secret interrogation facility of no return and only those in serious trouble were taken there. From the outside it did look a bit scary. High concrete T-walls ringed the compound making it look like a prison but in fact they were placed there to protect against shrapnel. Early on before we had the T-walls, a mortar had landed not far from our building and a piece of hot shrapnel ripped through the flimsy wooden walls barely missing us. Still hot when we picked it up we saved that jagged piece of metal to remind us of the danger of mortar attacks. Soon after, the Mayor Cell placed the ten foot high T-walls around us, to our great appreciation, but it gave the compound the added appearance of an impenetrable mini prison.

Khalif entered the compound and was immediately taken to an interview room a bit nervous like a kid who had done something wrong and thought his parents were on to him. He kept asking why he had been brought in for questioning. We tried to put him at ease explaining that it was routine for those who had been away for some time to visit us again for an update of their lives. I asked Khalif to simply explain what he done for the last three weeks and why he hadn't contacted us. Looking around as if he expected someone to sneak up behind him and hit him over the head, Khalif began with the story of how he went to the hospital for seven days and then recuperated at home the remainder of the time just thinking about all his personal problems. He said he had been having some stomach problems and needed rest. Putting him at ease we went over the information he supplied in his initial employment interview, covering the story about the trip to Syria and Khalif once again relayed identical information. He even added that while in Syria he visited several prostitutes, commenting that the women were good in Syria and cheap. He could stay all night with a woman there for a very small sum. All the other information in the initial interview appeared accurate but I was not comfortable with Khalif's reaction about his father and the trip to Syria. I questioned Khalif further and he said that he had not been back to Syria since and still had never seen his father in nine years. He did not know where his father was and no one in his family knew.

Suddenly, I remembered that Khalif had a friend working on base and I questioned him about the young man. Khalif said yes, his friend Hussein worked in the motor pool. Pausing the interview, I contacted motor pool and had Hussein brought to me for questioning.

Within 15 minutes Hussein was brought into another interview room out of sight of Khalif. Hussein did not seem overly worried about being called in. In fact, he seemed kind of happy go lucky, almost Pollyannaish. Tall and thin, Hussein was the same age as Khalif and confirmed he was Khalif's best friend since childhood. He characterized their relationship as even closer than a brother. As to Khalif's absence, Hussein confirmed that Khalif visited the hospital for a few days, but after that he traveled to Basra to see his father. Khalif's uncle, Ahmad, told Hussein the news and added that Khalif's father, Abdul, had given Khalif a large sum of money, but Hussein did not know how much exactly. Abdul gave the money to uncle Ahmad not for spending but for safekeeping by the uncle, a portion of it to be released to Khalif in increments. Hussein nonchalantly told of how a third friend of theirs, Ali, had actually made the trip with Khalif to Basra.

This was interesting. Khalif had told us a lie but either had not had time or didn't think it was necessary to inform his friends of the story. But why? Why lie about the trip to Basra or his father?

What was he hiding? To be fair we wanted to give Khalif another chance to tell the truth. We called Khalif back in and offered him a chance to change his story, but foolishly he maintained that he had not seen his father and did not travel outside of Baghdad at all the entire time. In fact, he claimed he went nowhere but his home and his aunt's home in Mosul. I became deeply concerned about the deception. It qualified as an automatic rejection of access to the base but I did not want this young man merely denied access to the FOB. The information was perishable and needed to be pursued before Khalif could discuss the issue with his friends.

Working with a local THT unit we teamed up for the interviews. Khalif was transferred for an overnight stay in the BIF keeping him incommunicado, while we interviewed Ali the next day. Young and naïve, Ali was a self-described life-long friend of Khalif and was worried about him. He told a slightly different, but even more interesting version of the story. Ali claimed that after release from the hospital, he and Khalif traveled not to Basra, as Hussein had related to us, but to Al Jawadi and Damascus, Syria where Khalif met his father. Ali said they left for Syria the same afternoon that Ali left the hospital and spent the entire time in Syria. For about two weeks Ali worked on a farm in Damascus to earn a few Dinars while Khalif spent most of the time back in Al Jawadi with his father and relatives. Ali knew nothing of any money the father might have given Khalif. A few times a week they would meet in the evening and spend time together drinking and visiting prostitutes. Khalif talked about how his father had acquired good connections in Syria that were helping him back in Iraq. Ali did not know what connections Khalif referred to but Khalif's father was making much more money because of them. Rather than be angry that Khalif was working for U.S. Forces, Khalif's father encouraged it. He instructed Khalif to return and try to gain the trust of the Americans.

The quick reaction and ability to follow-up on leads generated from the interviews allowed us to uncover Khalif's deception. He eventually admitted to four trips to Syria to see his father, who worked against Coalition Forces. Khalif could have continued working on MAF possibly gaining higher access through trust or may have gained information about U.S. Forces through meeting others in different positions on base. All that would have remained concealed had a sergeant who knew his men had not detected and reported something out of the ordinary to us and had we not acted on the perishable information immediately.

22 IRAQI POLICE

Much has been said in the U.S. media about the Iraqi
Police. As I wrote in an op-ed piece back in 2007, justifiably, there
had been much concern over the years about the state of the Iraqi
police force. A miserable history of desertion, subversion,
infiltration and corruption plagued the fledgling force from its
inception. Even considering the commendable progress in the
Kurdish areas, the Jones Commission, created to study the problem,
concluded that, "The Iraqi Police Service is incapable today of
providing security at a level to protect Iraqi neighborhoods from
insurgents and sectarian violence."[17] Sobering considering that on
paper we had trained 164,000 officers of which, the Defense
Department admitted in the report that somewhere between 30-60
percent had quit.

---

[17] Chaired by General James Jones, USMC (Ret.), the Independent
Commission on the Security Forces of Iraq reported to Congress in
September 2007 on the readiness of the Iraqi Security Forces, their
capabilities, and how support and training by U.S. forces contributes to the
effectiveness of the Iraqi Security Forces.

I contended and still contend that much of this longstanding problem was influenced by politics. In 2005, the U.S. military was asked to "screen" candidates for the Iraqi police force headed to Jordan for training. Pressed for time and the political demand for more officers on the street, quality took a seat far to the rear of quantity. What transpired was alarming. Within a short time it became apparent many candidates lacked the desire to become police officers but merely hoped to secure a steady paycheck. More troubling, a few were openly hostile toward government, both U.S. and Iraqi. Yes, there were a few good candidates, former military officers and college graduates among the group, but the bad apples sowed dissension. One of the American advisors told me that 85% of the police sympathized in some way with the insurgency. I found it hard to believe that the percentage was that high. He also mentioned that the police routinely cheered after hearing news that U.S. soldiers were killed.

A few persons certainly raised suspicions of being planted by sectarian militia or worse yet insurgent groups. Others might not have worked directly with militia or insurgents but would have been inclined to provide them information. As willful sympathizers within the force, they could inform insurgents of the numbers, types, and locations of weapons. The could also provide names of police personnel that could themselves become targets, or even operational data such as time and place of the next raid, or names of suspects or police targets could all become available to the enemy through this fifth column.

It was clear, even then, that more time and a sincere effort was needed to thoroughly screen candidates and weed out any who raised the slightest doubt as to loyalty or character. At the time, however, it was more important politically to plus up the numbers of trained police. Therefore, the notion of rejecting candidates was out. We were only permitted to conduct a cursory screening of the pitiful group of applicants. By the time of the Jones Commission report it appeared the process had not improved much. It took three wasted years and a blue ribbon panel to report what those on the ground complained about from the start; the process was flawed and driven by politics instead of mission requirements.

Apparently this was not new. In Ambassador Paul Bremer's book he documents a similar problem during his tenure. At one point in a tense meeting, questioning how the military was running up the numbers of police in training, Doug Brand, the senior advisor to the Interior Ministry replied that the Army was picking up "half-educated" men from the streets, putting them through 3 weeks of training, giving them weapons and then calling them "police." Simply put, it was a scandal.[18]

The Jones Commission suggested scrapping the current Iraqi force and starting anew. While seemingly unworkable in its entirety, the Commission was on to something. Iraq needs to create an elite police force unit, from within the ranks of the current one. Armed with increased authority and held to a much higher standard, it should be given a distinctive uniform and advertised as an elite force of integrity, justice and dedication to duty. This would appeal to idealistic Iraqis both young and old. Candidates would be subjected to a demanding selection process and rigorous vetting critical to the unit's ultimate success.

To help jumpstart the process, the U.S. needed seasoned CI agents to participate in the recruitment and training of the new Iraqi police, thoroughly pre-screening candidates, monitoring them through training and following up after assignment. Reliable vetting techniques were available and current databases used for background checks would need updating and modification, but it remained a workable solution. However, the government was not as interested in improving the process, as pumping out as many

---

[18] Bremer III, L. Paul. <u>My Year in Iraq.</u> (New York: Simon and Schuster, 2006), 183.

"trained" officers as fast as possible. This actually created more problems because the police force was so thoroughly infiltrated by dissidents and insurgents that they undermined the overall effectiveness of the entire force. Police could not work effectively if they could not trust those working in the same unit. Critical information could easily be compromised and honest officers' lives would be placed in danger. It only takes one or two in each unit to hamper the effectiveness of the entire cadre.

Iraq is full of principled young men eager to respond to a call of honor. Despite harassment, threats, assassinations and suicide attacks on recruits, young Iraqis consistently lined up for police duty. While they joined for a variety of reasons, some honorable, some nefarious, the goal should have remained helping Iraq select and train the most professional force possible. The question was whether Americans and Iraqis had the political will to properly build the kind of force that could earn the trust of the people and bring order to Iraq. The answer at the time was no.

Since then, Iraq continued to struggle with the problem. In September 2006, the New York Times reported internal security forces were actually blocking efforts to purge the Shiite militiamen and criminal elements that as the reporter stated, "were entrenched throughout the police." [19] For Iraqis to accomplish the needed purging themselves was next to impossible because of the sectarian hatred coupled with long memories of corruption under Saddam. Shiites do not want the police ever again controlled by Sunnis. The Interior Ministry discovered over 1,000 police and employees who had been convicted of murder, rape and robbery but had slipped through screening processes. Six months later, headlines screamed of Interior Ministry action to fire or reassign 10,000 police and high-ranking employees for ties to militia or criminal activity.[20] You have to give the Iraqis credit for trying but their best hope for solving this problem was allowing American CI agents to join forces with an elite cadre of Iraqis to screen and vet the police candidates.

---

[19] Wong, Edward and Paul von Zielbauer. "Iraq Stumbling in Bid to Purge its Rogue Police." New York Times. 17 Sept. 2006. 23 July 2008 <http://www.nytimes.com/2006/09/17/world/middleeast/17ministry.html?ex=1316145600&en=2093dc652ba69f59&ei=5090&partner=rssuserland&emc=rss>.

[20] Jervis, Rick. "Iraq Ousts 10,000 in Security Ministry," USA Today. 5 March 2007: 1.

23 PKK in Northern Iraq

When I saw news stories in 2007 of Turkey threatening to root out PKK terrorists in northern Iraq and the response of shock that these communist rebels had taken sanctuary there, it certainly reminded me of the scene in Casablanca where Humphrey Bogart's club is raided and the "shock" of the police that gambling was going on inside. The PKK is a Kurdish communist separatist group in eastern Turkey that has been hunted by the Turkish military for decades. It was an open secret that the PKK frequented Kurdish territory in northern Iraq. We had picked up plenty of intelligence from Kurdish and Turkish workers about the Turkish military pursuing them there. In fact, the PKK had probably never really left since they first received permission to operate from there in 1982 from Iraq's Kurdistan Democratic Party (KDP).[21] It was so well

---

[21] For more on this see Marcus, Aliza. Blood and Belief: The PKK and the Kurdish Fight for Independence. (New York: New York University Press, 2007), 69.

266

known that we were told to stop reporting it in intelligence channels.

As I said earlier, the Kurdish nation is a unique group of people some experts say number about 30 million but Kurds say number closer to 60 million. Their proud history goes back to famous warriors like Saladin who captured Jerusalem from the crusaders. But they have always seemed to be a pawn for larger nations in the region. Kurds remain a stateless nation covering parts of northern Iraq, eastern Turkey, western Iran and northeastern Syria. None of the countries bordering Iraq want to see the establishment of a Kurdish state for fear of the turmoil it will cause in their countries. Kurds in Turkey suffered prejudice and persecution eventually spawning groups like the PKK who fought unsuccessfully for decades trying to gain a separate state in the rugged mountains of eastern Turkey. The Turkish government drove them out and instituted programs to assimilate Kurds as Turks. This worked well for Turkey and the PKK lost much of its popular support but not all. They fight on but the odd fact was the majority of Turkish Kurds really did not want to fight for a separate nation, most just wanted the Turks to stop discriminating against them. I talked to a middle aged Kurd from Turkey with a visible anger against Turkey for discrimination against the Kurds. Openly he talked about a few of his cousins who at one time joined an arm of the PKK HADEP[22] party and was forced to leave Turkey. But the vast majority of the hundreds, maybe thousands, I came across would not fight for independence. They might accept independence if it came but were simply not willing to fight for it. A large number of Turkish Kurds could not even speak Kurdish well and some could not speak Kurdish at all. They had already integrated into Turkish society.

Iraqi Kurds have come closest to forming their own country. Kurds proudly fly the flag of Kurdistan in their part of Iraq and have a working government providing excellent security which has brought foreign investment and prosperity to the region. America has been a strong supporter although we failed them after the first Gulf War when we expected them to rise up and overthrow Saddam but failed to assist the Kurds when Saddam lashed out at them. Kurds still count Americans as their friends and certainly within Iraq they are our closest ally.

---

[22] HADEP stands for Halkin Demokrasi Partisi which in Turkish means Peoples Democratic Party. It was an authorized Kurdish party formed in 1994 but later banned by Turkish courts in 2003.

24 U.S. CONTRACTORS

Civilian contractors fulfill an important role in Iraq performing all kinds of tasks from construction, transportation, food service, trash removal, translation, security and intelligence to name just a few. In theory, the government, mainly the military, receives a good deal in return. Although contractors' wages are extremely high they are employed a short time and can be dismissed at the will of the government. They provide needed experience to a young military force freeing soldiers to perform the war-fighting mission. Without contractors, the military would have to either recruit more soldiers or more government civilians. Recruiting more soldiers is certainly politically undesirable but moreover, it might not even be possible without a draft. Hiring more government civilians is also not desirable because once hired, it is very difficult to draw down the force after a conflict has ended.

In the short run (three to five years), civilian contractors can be an economical force multiplier for the military. The biggest problem with civilian contractors is lack of military supervision. The Army is still defining how to use contractors effectively. Even seemingly small problems can become an irritant. For example, what government civilian grade equivalent should contractors receive, if any? These are highly paid individuals, many well over $120,000 per year. Contactors argue they should be afforded high GS equivalents such as GS-13 through 15. I argue this is similar to awarding them military ranks of Colonel and General and should not be done. The government has failed to even require a standard among contractors. A few of the CI agents who worked for me were assigned GS equivalents of 12. Meanwhile, a few of the interpreters who worked under us were assigned 13s. This caused conflict at the working level. As one example, the grade difference meant that the terps were authorized government quarters to themselves while the CI agents by regulation were required to double up. All this while U.S. Army Captains and Majors were required to double up or even sleep three to a room. It is hard to justify having an interpreter with single quarters while the key officers are sharing. Other working level problems were numerous. The Army needs to develop a contractor rank system including commensurate benefits due them for housing and transportation.

Finally, while I saw a reasonable percentage of qualified personnel among contractors, there were far too many poorly qualified or troublesome contractors. Even considering the high salaries, it was difficult for companies to convince enough good employees to serve in Iraq. This posed a continuing problem of recruiting less than desirable employees and keeping others that should have been relieved of duty.

With the scandal involving Blackwater security in 2007, contractors gained a bad reputation. Whether or not one gives the benefit of the doubt to Blackwater, scores of contractors used the war to their advantage to make money at the expense of the mission. National news sources are replete with stories of fraud, corruption, and failure to deliver products as stated, not to mention the kinds of accusations of unreasonable force levied in the Blackwater example.

I saw firsthand the types of fraud against the U.S. taxpayer ignored by Army officials and exploited by civilian companies. In the fog of war, money wasted is not the priority of the military, winning the war is the priority, and rightly so. My complaint was it would have taken nothing away from the war-fighting mission to correct some of the glaring examples of fraud, waste and abuse perpetrated by companies. In fact, it was a responsibility they should have shouldered themselves, because it is not right to cheat the American people. One simple case involved payment to contractors for hours not worked.

Intelligence and interpreter contracts specified seven-day 12 hours per day schedules for the bulk of its employees. Contract wages were negotiated and calculated on that schedule and the salaries were not cheap. Interpreters could make over $100,000 per year and Intelligence Specialists closer to $140,000. That did not include benefits, which could add another $20,000 per year. That figure included salary only, for each employee the company charged the government almost twice that amount to cover overhead and

271

expenses. Such exorbitant salaries were based on that 12-hour per day seven-day per week schedule. In actuality, few employees worked 12 hours per day or seven days per week. Most worked eight-hour days, six days per week or less. When I arrived in Mosul, employees were working four to six hours per day, five days per week. No one really supervised them; they supervised themselves. It took a major shake-up to get the crew back on a schedule of 12 hours per day. But when I called around to other units, few of them worked such hours. This amounted to millions of dollars in overspent money from the taxpayers. Though I pointed this out in writing through the Army Inspector General and the Contracting Officer's Representative (COR), I don't know of any action taken to correct the issue.

Systematic lack of supervision allowed contractors to operate this way. In the case of the intelligence contractor, multiple subcontractors supplied personnel to the prime contractor. Each subcontractor used its own time sheet and corresponding system for tracking billable hours to the government. Some contractors actually completed the time sheets for their employees back at corporate headquarters in America. We were told never to submit less than 12 hours per day, as that would affect the billable hours. We were also told that if the military authorized time off we could still bill the hours. I agree, most military units offer a day off each week and people in a combat zone generally need a day off. However, the taxpayer should not be charged for that day. The taxpayer was and is billed for millions of dollars in un-worked hours. By allowing this to continue we have institutionalized fraud.

There were simple fixes for this problem but they were not instituted. First, the Army could have required a local military officer to verify and sign contractor time sheets, and copies should have been kept for audit purposes. All the contractors worked for a military person somewhere in the chain. We used this process in my office and it compelled the military to hold contractors accountable. Major White signed our time sheets and there was no way he would sign for hours not worked. No officer wants to sign a time sheet for hours not worked so he ensures the unit works the required hours. Second, from time to time the Defense Contract Audit Agency should have audited contractor hours and methodology. I never saw such an audit while I was in Iraq, although I heard they conducted a partial audit years before. Third, the military could have designated one standard time sheet for the contract. Finally, the contract should have been negotiated for six-day workweeks with pay adjusted accordingly. Implementation of the seven-day weeks could have been left to meet mission requirements as needed. Such a system would have allowed employees time off that was not billable to the taxpayer.

Another serious problem with contractors was the lack of a disciplinary system. Incredibly, employees who developed problems, violated military regulations, or even committed criminal acts were handled internally by the contractor. This constituted a blatant conflict-of–interest and allowed the contractor to cover-up or mitigate criminal as well as operational difficulties. The contractor had a clear financial interest not to fire persons, which directly conflicted with the best interests of the U.S. Government. I saw this play out numerous times during my tour. One case in particular, a contract employee committed multiple General Order #1 violations, including possessing three unauthorized machine guns and ammunition, but the company management transferred the employee from one unit and promoted him to a higher position in another part of the country even after a complete investigation by Security Police. The reason given was that the company was shorthanded and forced to pay penalties for unfilled slots, thus it could not afford to fire people regardless of their actions. As this person's former supervisor, I provided a written statement to the company that the employee was unfit to work in counterintelligence in a position of trust and responsibility. From the beginning, the country manager for the company tried to cover up and mitigate the offenses. He also implemented a gag order on employees, forbidding them to discuss it further with him or with the military. In my opinion, there was a reasonable argument that the company was willing to sacrifice the safety and security involved in the CI mission to save the company from losing money. Many persons, not in positions of trust, had been sent home for possession of a single bottle of alcohol, also a violation of General Order #1. This case was far more serious and was purposely covered up. All persons under this contract were "at will" employees and could be relieved without cause at any time, but the company refused.

In another case, an interpreter, who was identified as falsifying translations at two locations, was merely reassigned instead of terminated. In my opinion, the interpreter contractor repeatedly cut corners, ultimately sacrificing security of the forces for the sake of money.

This type of activity can be quite serious as in the May 2008 story of Iraqi employees at the British embassy complaining that they were coerced to perform sexually for elements of the American Contractor KBR or face reductions in pay, harassment or termination. Once again, KBR was left to investigate itself, which is always a bad idea.[23]

Once again, the fixes for this were simple. To preserve the integrity of the system, a military JAG and or General Officer should review contractor violations for appropriate command action. Secondly, require military or COR as command action authority on any investigation of contractor employees. A party representing the government's interest should be the action

---

[23] Haynes, Deborah and Sonia Verma. "Iraqis allege sex abuse at the British Embassy." Times Online. 8 May 2008. 24 July 2008 <http: //www.timesonline.co.uk/tol/news/world/iraq/article3890121.ece>.

authority, not the contractor. An alternative would be to require the first 0-5 in the contractor's military chain to act as command action authority on the contractor.

A third area of improvement involved hiring approval. Because the COR ultimately approves the resumes for all contract employees, the onus to hire the BEST people is transferred from the contractor to the COR. The thrust from the contractor became, "we can hire whomever; as long as the COR approves the resume, we are exempt from responsibility for the backgrounds of our employees." With both the intelligence and interpreter contractors desperate to fill slots, resumes were not checked thoroughly by the contractor. Applicants with prior discipline and poor performance on this contract, which would otherwise disqualify them, were too often not identified, and subsequently hired. Without proper background information, the COR unwittingly approved unsuitable applicants based on only a resume. Military representatives relied on the integrity of the contractor for the accuracy of the resumes. The contract should include penalties to the contractor for providing employees with troubled backgrounds that should have reasonably been detected by the contractor, and the COR should be even more vigilant in scrutinizing new hires.

One of the most famous cases made public involved a naturalized Muslim citizen operating under multiple aliases who was sentenced to 13 years in prison in 2007 for illegally possessing classified information. Allegedly he passed information to Iraqi insurgents that may have brought harm to hundreds of U.S. soldiers and Iraqi civilians. One public commentary noted: How did we let this counterintelligence debacle occur with such disastrous results? The short answer was Titan's screening program for local personnel in Iraq enabled infiltration through ineffective and unprofessional background investigations. When information gathered by professional counterintelligence linguists/analysts was presented to U.S. military commanders pointing this out, it was sloughed off.[24]

A recommended fix that works would involve insisting that contractors perform due diligence on resumes. If a resume is approved by COR and problems are later discovered, the contractor should be responsible. This will force contractors to scrutinize the applicants more closely.

The bottom line to the contractor problems in these areas lay at the feet of poor organization. Chain of command was not properly instituted. In the case of the intelligence contract, both operational and administrative control of the contractors was maintained by the C-2, a staff intelligence officer. As a rule, staff functions do not exercise operational control over line operations.

---

[24] Gordon, Jerry. "An Intelligence Disaster in Iraq," WorldNetDaily. 1 March 2007. 23 July 2008 <http://worldnetdaily.com/news/article.asp?ARTICLE_ID=54491>.

C-2 could not effectively supervise CI teams working in numerous locations throughout the AOR. C-2 should have maintained administrative control over the units and local commanders, whom the units supported, should have had clear operational control.

Local military commanders in general, did not understand the authority they held over contractors and thus failed to control contractors properly. This resulted in lower productivity and reduced mission accomplishment. In Mosul, the Base Commander and Force Protection Officer instituted an effective system that resulted in the most productive operations in northern Iraq. Local military commanders must understand the relationship between the military unit (as a customer) and the contractor. Military commanders have a right to demand productive and responsive service. Commanders need to know they have the authority to hold the contractor accountable and in fact have an obligation to do so.

Finally, I recommend the COR maintain direct lines of communication with servicing unit commanders. Contractors do not inform the COR about poor performing employees or those with trouble unless absolutely necessary. The local military commander should have a direct line to the COR to report these matters. Military commanders need to know that they have a direct line to the COR and an obligation to supervise and report non-performers and those with discipline problems. Bottom line: contractors need thorough supervision and auditing.

25 U.S. MILITARY

Though our military is the finest the world has ever
produced, in some areas it performs at only a shadow of the
greatness it could achieve. Like any large organization, it is
shackled by bureaucracy, by methods that simultaneously
strengthen it and limit its potential. It is also fraught with political
correctness as much as its members fight such inclinations. In a war
zone, other difficulties besiege the force that are less noticeable
during peace. Basically, soldiers serve in Iraq on one-year tours,
sometimes extended. The Air Force is the exception and chooses to
send most of its members on shorter temporary assignments. The
one-year tour syndrome produces a "reinventing the wheel" effect to
a large extent. A unit arrives in Iraq, enjoys a two-week turnover
with the unit it replaces. They perform what is known as "the right
seat ride" for one week watching the outgoing unit closely
observing its methods. Units switch roles the second week allowing
the incoming unit to take over operations with the outgoing unit
observing to answer questions and ensure the transition runs
smoothly. After that, the incoming unit is on its own, usually
without the benefit of the experience and knowledge of the previous
unit. Though unit members may face most of the same problems,

the new unit must decide how to deal with those problems and craft its own solutions. Unit members become proficient at this after about three to six months and work efficiently for the next four or five months. Then they develop an attitude of looking forward to returning home and begin to defer certain actions until their replacements arrive. Within a month the replacements enter country and the right seat ride process starts all over again. This cycle of "learning then leaving" was repeated throughout the occupation and was not new to Iraq. We have had over fifty years of it in places like South Korea so the Army is quite familiar with the notion.

Here I want to address the way the Army treats counterintelligence. In the civilian government the FBI handles criminal matters and counterintelligence. The CIA is a foreign intelligence gathering organization, in essence the spies. Within the Army, criminal matters are investigated by the CID and counterintelligence is designated as part of Military Intelligence. The Air Force organizes itself along civilian lines. In the Army, MI is a large function tasked with collecting information on the enemy. CI ends up as an afterthought in the intelligence bureaucracy rendering CI ineffective in training, authority and effectiveness. The Army needs to separate its CI function completely from MI. The CI function is an investigative/slash defensive intelligence function that is far better carried out by investigators. Army specialties have endured changes and specialization for interrogation, analysts and investigators. All of these tasks are natural to investigators and would be better placed in either CID or in a Special CI Command.

As I stated earlier, U.S. Army CI agents don't receive the law enforcement training or experience that would prove useful in a situation like Iraq where U.S. soldiers take civilians into custody. Investigation, evidence collection, and interrogation in this context should fall to CI agents assigned to individual units or to the base Force Protection. The U.S. Army is not organized in this manner. While CI agents in the Army currently only have law enforcement authority pertaining to espionage type criminal activity, they do not have the broad criminal experience of FBI or USAF investigators that would be helpful in a counterinsurgency situation.

Final Thoughts

I hope I successfully provided interesting insight to the war inside the wire and how our forces wage it. Both duty assignments I experienced in Iraq were unforgettable experiences where I felt able to contribute to the mission while working with some of the finest men and women in my entire military and civilian careers. Not enough credit is given to these war fighters, and as I have pointed out, we need to improve our methods of operation. My best to all those I served with and to those who continue to serve our country every day selflessly.

ACKNOWLEDGMENTS

I want to thank the men and women of the 114th ALT whom I served with at Abu Ghraib prison especially my good friend Hiram Dahmer and the Commander, Colonel Robert Thomas, as well as the Marines who helped protect all of us. In Mosul I want to thank all my comrades from 2/180th Field Artillery (Forward). I can't name them all but let me include Jason Swope, who spent tireless hours perfecting our security systems, and doing whatever it took to catch the "bad guys," Lt Col. Jeffrey Tipton, who provided outstanding leadership and support to the CI mission, standing up to higher headquarters when we were right and providing me with whatever resources I needed, and Lt. Col Rob White who was the ramrod that allowed us to implement innovative ways to neutralize the enemy and win the war inside the wire. I also want to mention Bret Bradshaw who came late to the fight but jumped in and contributed greatly to the total effort.

LIST OF ABBREVIATIONS

Abbreviation / page first appears

AIF	Anti-Iraqi Forces	pg 178
AOR	Area of Responsibility	pg 45
BIF	Battalion Interrogation Facility	pg 189
BOLO	Be on Lookout for	pg 216
CAC	Common Access Card	pg 209
CI	Counterintelligence	pg 4
CID	Criminal Investigations Division	pg 195
COR	Contracting Officer's Representative	pg 272
CPA	Coalition Provisional Authority	pg 196
CPATT	Civilian Police Advisory Training Team	pg 210
CTC	Chinese Telegraphic Code	pg 58
DFAC	Dining Facility	pg 2
DIF	Division Interrogation Facility	pg 89
DOD	Department of Defense	pg 209
ECP	Entry Control Point	pg 23
FOB	Forward Operating Base	pg 2
FPS	Facilities Protection Service	pg 133
GS	General Schedule	pg 211
HET	Human Exploitation Team	pg 50
HUMINT	Human Intelligence	pg 63
ICO	Iraqi Correction Officers	pg 20
IED	Improvised Explosive Device	pg 13

IHA	Interrogation Holding Area	pg 37
IIR	Intelligence Information Report	pg 215
ING	Iraqi National Guard	pg 248
KBR	Kellogg Brown and Root	pg 42
KDP	Kurdistan Democratic Party	pg 133
LEP	Locally Employed Person	pg 185
LN	Local National	pg 207
MAF	Mosul Air Field	pg 116
MCT	Movement Control Team	pg 6
MI	Military Intelligence	pg 51
MP	Military Police	pg 20
MNF-I	Multi National Force Iraq	pg 196
OSD	Office of Secretary of Defense	pg 53
Peshmerga	Kurdish Freedom Fighters	pg 90
PKK	Turkish Kurdish terrorist group	pg 167
PUK	Patriotic Union of Kurdistan	pg 133
PX	Post Exchange	pg 208
QRF	Quick Reaction Force	pg 37
SES	Senior Executive Service	pg 213
SF	Special Forces	pg 99
TFF	Task Force Freedom	pg 116
THT	Tactical HUMINT Team	pg 63
TOC	Tactical Operations Center	pg 192
TTP	Tactics, Techniques and Procedures	pg 161
VBIED	Vehicle Borne Improvised Explosive Device	pg 225

ABOUT THE AUTHOR

Dr. Richard Saccone was born and raised near Pittsburgh, Pennsylvania. He earned his academic degrees from Weber State University (B.S.), Naval Postgraduate School (M.A.), University of Oklahoma (M.P.A.), and the University of Pittsburgh (Ph.D.). He spent a career as a counterintelligence and counterespionage officer in the USAF and served one year in Iraq as a Senior Counter-intelligence Agent in charge of a HUMINT Support Team.

Dr. Saccone has dealt with hostile intelligence threats in Asia and the Middle East. He has visited, lived and worked in over 50 countries including six in the Middle East. He now teaches International Relations, Global Terrorism and Political Science at St. Vincent College in Latrobe, PA.

2235396

Made in the USA